# Ever Heard of Her?

Women of Achievement To Know …
and Why You Don't

By Lisa Savage

Illustrations by Ruby Pfeifle

*Lisa Savage*

Industry Books | Beverly Farms, MA

2020 Industry Books LLC

Copyright © 2020 by Lisa Savage

Illustrations © 2020 by Ruby Pfeifle

Library of Congress Cataloging-in-Publication Data

Savage, Lisa.

Ever heard of her: women of achievement to know ... and why you don't / by Lisa Savage.

p. cm.

ISBN 97817356912061495

1. Women. 2. Notoriety. 3. Human Rights. 4. Achievement.

Printed in the United States of America

Industry Books web site: www.RealBookShop.com

Book design by Mark Sayer

## *Dedication*

To both my grandmothers and my mother, who showed me firsthand what women could do.

# Contents

## *About the Author*

Lisa Savage, at the time of this publication, is an independent Green candidate for U.S. Senate in Maine. Public service and working for peace and justice have been a way of life. Savage sees working for the common good as the least she can do for the great opportunity she has been provided here in Maine, including the amazing community of people who supported her family's small business in Skowhegan.

Twenty-five years ago, Savage turned to teaching, working in the public schools primarily with students from low-income families. And as an elected vice president and chief negotiator for her unit of the Maine Education Association, she worked tirelessly to make sure teachers got the money, benefits, and job security they deserved for their hard work.

Now a grandmother four times, Savage and her husband, Mark Roman, a woodworker, are acutely aware of the challenges faced by the Millennial generation. Their five grown children all live and work in other states, largely due to student debt and the scarcity of good-paying jobs close to home. This fuels her efforts to preserve the future — to make Maine and the United States live up to the promises built into our Constitution: Life, liberty, and the pursuit of happiness.

You can learn more about her campaign at www.lisaformaine.org.

# Introduction

## Never Heard of Her?

### Why Many Women of Achievement Aren't Remembered

Introduction by Janet Weil, research collaborator

*"Anonymous was a woman."* - *proverb*

This book, started, as many books do, with a conversation:

A friend saying to Lisa, "There are so many amazing women who are unknown besides the women in *Hidden Figures* …"

Lisa: "Maybe you should write a book about that."

Friend: "Oh, I could never do such a huge project!"

Lisa: "Maybe you need a team …"

And here we are.

As we began work on *Ever Heard of Her?* we asked ourselves: Which women of achievement don't "we" (meaning the general adult public, including ourselves) know about? By "know about" we intend the kind of popular familiarity with names and basic information that most adults remember about men of achievement. And most importantly, what is lost when we never hear of these women?

We wondered: How will we choose from the dozens of women of achievement we found in preliminary searches? Our friends and acquaintances helped. We sent out a long list of worthy names with the simple question: Ever heard of her? The most common reply: "I am ashamed to say I don't know who any of these women are."

After we chose the women for our book we looked at their stories and asked: What does this tiny sample of women of achievement tell us about the loss to everyone when we don't learn about their discoveries and accomplishments?

Where are they absent? Symphonic orchestra programs, lists of "The Greatest…," art museum collections, public libraries, textbooks, political talk shows, city walking tours, the History Channel — and the obituaries of *The New York Times*?

Then the harder question: Why? Why don't we know them?

*Ever Heard of Her?* explores the question of gender equity in terms of robust, lasting popular recognition and fame for women. This book focuses on the gap between men's and women's visibility and legacies in mainstream media, cultural programming, and popular histories including biographies.

Our wondering about who we have "never heard of" evokes a paradox. How do we notice absence and silence, the obscure, the name in the footnotes only, the unnamed lone woman in the group photo? How do we confront and start to correct the many failures of collective memory, popular media, and the public/historical record?

In the 21st century, the "Age of Information," women have been working and achieving in the public sphere for a long time. Barriers to our participation in sports, the professions, elected office, academia, the military and the arts have been falling, our political power and public presence accelerating, since the 1960s. So why have we "heard of" men so much more than women? With the ever-increasing flood of information — visual, auditory and textual — available, the idea that a vast amount of significant human achievement goes unrecognized seems … unlikely.

Similar to the remark, "Well, if I can't remember what I was going to say, it couldn't have been very important!," the line, "Well, if I never heard of them, or can't remember them, how important could they be?," may come to mind.

Here's a quick thought experiment. Track and field may or may not have been your sport in college, but you have heard of _____ . Whatever you think about climate change, you have probably read or heard something on the subject by _____ . Like or dislike American symphonic music, you've listened to music composed by _____ . If you've watched documentaries on U.S. foreign policy, surveillance, whistleblowing and wars, you recognize the names _____ , _____ , _____ . Asked to name a Latinx labor organizer, you'd probably say _____ . When you are working on a crossword puzzle with a clue about the polio vaccine, you have little to no trouble coming up with _____ . Chatting about 20th century American painters, _____ , _____ , _____ , or maybe _____ drop into your conversation. People whose names you know who have done important writing and advocacy for the victims of atrocities probably include _____ , _____ , or _____ . Being asked about Native American leaders may give you pause, as their history is the most erased of all, but it's likely you can answer, depending on where you live, with _____ , _____ , _____ , or _____ .

Did you put in any women's names in the blanks? Or did you try - but come up empty? Or did the men's names come so quickly to mind that all the blanks "just happened" to be filled with them?

If so, don't feel bad — or alone. You've come to the right book.

The blanking out of the record of women's achievement is sometimes deliberate, a product of malicious sexism, racism, and/or xenophobic nationalism, and we examine cases of that in this book. But mostly it happens because of the unconscious bias of both men and women, leading us to regard men as "achievers," "leaders," "experts," especially in fields which have been coded male, such as the sciences, the military, or sports, and to neglect the contributions of women. It's an intersectional failure of remembering and honoring women of color.

It may be useful to think in terms of a metaphor.

Imagine a mountain trail. At the fairly flat and wide trailhead, a multitude of young and sometimes not-young women assemble. These are the students, the interns, the junior staffers, the amateurs or beginners with "an interest" in some field or endeavor. They have energy and promise, aptitude and ambition.

The trail gradually narrows. Some of the women go on to grad school. Some pursue careers, and some take what jobs they can find, hoping for better later. Some get support: a big push over boulders or across streams, clear guidance for the trail, friendly nods from women further up the trail.

Others drop out. Some are diverted onto cul-de-sacs and mean to rejoin the trail later — after having a child or after other family commitments, unpaid and uncredited in the work world.

Some rejoin the trail later. Some have remarkable careers and successes late in life.

Some are pushed roughly off the trail. Some fall by the wayside, exhausted, with no attention, as if they had never been there.

Many find a plateau and do good (or great) work and are content. Some are bitter, filled with regret at not having achieved what they knew they were capable of, or not having gotten credit for their accomplishments, or knowing their work will not be preserved in libraries, museums, historical records, popular culture.

The trail becomes very narrow and steep. The few remaining women are encouraged not to look back, not to help each other, and not to make way for others. Great rewards await those who have made it to the high altitudes, but often also loneliness, workaholism, chronic stress.

The summit is their legacy: continuing public recognition, even fame, after death. This is the narrowest place of all.

Few women's ghosts rest on that summit. It helps to have been closely connected to a man or men (husbands, lovers, promoters, directors, writers) on the much wider and higher summit for male achievement. It helps to have been white and/or rich, achieved greatness in the performing arts or fashion, had great beauty or talent, enjoyed the sustained support of male colleagues, and/or have died tragically. We are in no danger of forgetting Marilyn or Jackie or Aretha.

Where are all the others, the ones whose achievements and lives were part of their time, and our common human story? They are not even forgotten, for the most part — we never knew about them in the first place. How little the achievements of living women receive public recognition and media attention, outside of women's professional fields or community/activist networks (sometimes not even then).

When a traveling timeline exhibit to accompany the book *Her Story: A Timeline of the Women Who Changed America* made the rounds in 2008, the authors observed: "Every person who views the exhibit comments about how much history he or she did not learn in school and never knew anything about."

As you read the individual women's chapters, notice the barriers first to entering, or continuing in, the occupation of each woman's choice, and/or the obstacles to her achievements being recognized publicly and recorded in history.

These nine women's records of achievement broke through to some extent, or we would not have the material to write about them. But the difficult questions persist: how much of a woman's fame is written on water, and why?

What to do about it is the subject of our conclusion.

# Ever Heard of Her?

# CHAPTER ONE

1

# "Tuskegee Flash":
# ALICE COACHMAN (1923-2014)

*"They [boys] would say, You can't beat me! Oh yes, I can!"*

In 1948, a track star from Georgia sailed across the Atlantic to London where she would finally be able to compete in the Olympic Games. The 1940 and 1944 summer games had been cancelled due to to the global war that was raging. Alice Coachman remembers preparing to set a world record in the high jump: "There were 85,000 people staring at me. In a big crowd and competition, you don't hear a thing. It's very quiet." The record she set that day held for the next eight years, and it made Coachman the first African-American woman to win an Olympic gold medal.

Ever heard of her?

## *Segregated in Victory*

Though she had just received a gold medal presented by King George VI of England, her victory celebration back home was segregated. Coachman remembered a motorcade with people lining the roads to greet her upon her return to the U.S. and then, "We marched into the Albany (GA) Municipal Auditorium. The Blacks were on the left. The whites were on the right." None of the white people in town signed the cards that accompanied flowers delivered to her home, or a gift certificate townsfolk had contributed to from a jewelry store in town. "To come back home to your own country, your own state and your own city, and you can't get a handshake from the mayor? Wasn't a good feeling," Coachman said in an interview for the National Visionary Leader Project now archived in the Library of Congress American Folklife Center.

Not everyone was so petty. Coachman was congratulated in person by President Harry Truman and former first lady Eleanor Roosevelt. Also, celebrated Black bandleader Count Basie held a reception for her, which was probably a special thrill as she had once aspired to be as famous as he was. Coachman would listen to Basie's band on her father's radio. She later reminisced:

> "I wanted to blow sax like Coleman Hawkins. Ooooo-ey. I wanted to be on the stage like Shirley Temple. I *never* thought I would be famous for running track.
>
> "No one ever sat down and told me what the Olympics were about. I was quiet, unassuming, not the type to ask questions. I wouldn't do that to a child now. I'd let them know what it's all about."

# *Tuskegee Flash*

Though her parents had been skeptical about her childhood athletic pursuits, the encouragement of her aunt Carry Spry and her 5th grade teacher Cora Bailey helped her persevere. Expectations for a girl's behavior were also an obstacle that Coachman sailed over. Her family expected daughters to be "ladylike" and sit quietly on the porch when their chores were done. She was often punished because, "I was kind of a tomboy."

Sexism played a part in motivating Coachman to compete in school. In 4th grade on the playground, she remembered how it was:

> "The boys would say, 'You can't beat me.'

> "And I would say, 'Oh yes I can! ... You'll bully me, that I can't jump that? That I can't outjump you? Uh uh, not me (shaking her head) Not me.'"

Her long training for victory was segregated, too. Most of the track meets of her childhood did not welcome her as a Black girl. Most of her opportunities for training were separate and unequal, like tying rags together to make a hurdle and running barefoot down dirt roads.

By the time she was competing as a member of the track team at Madison High School, scouts for Tuskegee Institute High School were ready to offer a scholarship to the 16-year-old star.

"I had to work my way through high school and college," said Coachman. "I can't remember 50 cents my parents gave me ... I was on my own." She cleaned the pool and mended the football uniforms, among other tasks. "Plus I sang in the choir." Asked when she found time to study, Coachman said, "You need my roommate to tell you, I would go to sleep with the book right here," that is, on her chest as she fell asleep reading. Her roommate, who called her "Slim," kept her choir uniform clean and wrinkle-free for her. "She says, 'Slim, sleep.'" The choir kept her going through her worry about her mother and how she was managing at home without Coachman's help.

Coachman had played basketball on a team that won three conference championships for Tuskegee, a historically Black school in Alabama. She became a sprinter with the nickname "Tuskegee Flash," and with excellent coaching and support for women's track and field she won national championships for 50-yard and 100-yard dashes and the 4 x 100 relay. Offering teens the opportunity to develop as scholar-athletes, Tuskegee filled an important role in Coachman's development, as it did for many Black girl athletes during that time. *Olympic Black Women* author Martha Ward Plowden wrote:

> "Her performance in the national Amateur Athletic Union (AAU) meets for Tuskegee Institute contributed to its reputation in women's track and field. The Tuskegee Relays were the proving ground for many young African-American females in the south."

Two of her coaches, Christine Evans Petty and Cleveland Abbott, were inducted into the Tuskegee University Athletic Hall of Fame in the 1970s. As an alumna of Tuskegee, Coachman is in good company; it is the alma mater of Betty Shabazz, George Washington Carver, and Martin Luther King Jr. Tuskegee also prepared her to enter Albany (GA) State College where she earned a bachelor's degree in 1949. Later, the city of Albany named Alice Avenue after her.

## *Missing Her Peak*

The rise of white nationalism in Europe changed the course of Coachman's athletic career by denying her two Olympics. "It's a long time from 1939 to 1948," she said. "In '44, I was really ready; I was at my peak. I know I could have won at least two gold medals."

Meanwhile, she kept busy, winning the national high jump championship for 10 years in a row with her unusual style, plus 25 national track and field championships in other events. She explained later, "Track and field was my key to getting a degree and meeting great people and opening a lot of doors."

Coachman set an American and Olympic record for her high jump of 5 feet 6⅛ inches at age 25. "I've always believed that I could do whatever I set my mind to do," she told a reporter for *Essence* in 1984.

## *Life After the Olympics*

Coachman also made a conscious choice to postpone love and marriage until after her gold medal win. She told a newspaper reporter in 1995:

> "I had accomplished what I wanted to do. It was time for me to start looking for a husband. That was the climax — I won the gold medal. I proved to my mother, my father, my coach, and everybody else that I had gone to the end …"

After she retired from competition, Coachmen became a teacher and coach, describing herself as willing to do pretty much anything that would help a child. Her degree in home economics with a minor in science from Albany State helped her gain faculty positions at South Carolina State College and two of her alma maters: Tuskegee Institute, and Albany State. She also raised two children, a son and a daughter.

She also established the Alice Coachman Track and Field Foundation (now defunct) to help youngsters and also former Olympic athletes who were struggling economically. Not every competitor could count on receiving an endorsement deal like Coachman signed with Coca-Cola in 1952, appearing in an international ad campaign with fellow Olympic track and field medalist Jesse Owens.

## *Making — and Correcting — History*

In 1996 the modern Olympics celebrated its centennial year, and Coachman found herself among the 100 former Olympians honored at the games held in Atlanta, Georgia. The previous year she had been recognized by the Avon cosmetics company in a New York exhibit "The Olympic Woman," where she joined other notables like Joan Benoit Samuelson, the first woman to win a gold medal in the marathon. Interviewed by William Rhoden for the *New York Times*, Coachman passed on some maternal wisdom about handling fame:

> "From the very first gold medal I won in 1939, my mama used to stress being humble. You're no better than anyone else. The people you pass on the ladder will be the same people you'll be with when the ladder comes down."

Laura J. Bruch interviewed Coachman in 1996 for the *Philadelphia Inquirer*:

> "'I had this dream. I wanted to do this,'' Coachman, who lives in Tuskegee, Ala., said recently on a trip to Philadelphia to attend the Alice Coachman/Paul Robeson Field Day, sponsored annually by Health Partners for the city's public schools. 'I wanted my story to get out ... to let people know what a struggle I had.'''

In 1996 Coachman told Jay Weiner of the *Minneapolis Star Tribune*, "Television has played a very important part in bringing things to light. You go any place and people will tell you Wilma

Rudolph was the first Black woman to win a medal. It's not true. She came on the scene 12 years later. But she was on television."

But some people do remember. She was inducted into the USA Track & Field Hall of Fame in 1975, and the U.S. Olympic Hall of Fame in 2004. Sportswriter Paul Newberry covered her story for the Associated Press. *The Oregonian* ran his article with the headline, "IT WAS COACHMAN WHO MADE HISTORY." An excerpt from the 1996 interview:

> "Many times I've been to places where I'll tell them I was the first Black woman to win an Olympic gold medal and they'll look at me like I'm crazy," she said, a tinge of astonishment in her voice. They'll say, `You won it? No, you didn't win it. It was that other girl who won it.'"

## *Analysis*

So, how come you never heard of Alice Coachman? Racism, particularly as manifested in the white-male-dominated sports journalism of the time, made Coachman's moment of fame fleeting, indeed. Also, female athletics had a long way to come in the years after she won the Olympic gold. And then there's socio-economic class. Olympic athletes representing the United States today typically come from upper middle class or wealthy families who can afford the training and equipment to pursue a sport to its highest level, or to send a child to an elite university with a top notch sports program. Coachman sailed over these barriers on talent and perseverance, but her fame was fleeting.

Unlike for track star Jesse Owens, no biopic has (yet) been made of her eventful life, perhaps in part because her story does not lend itself to the always-popular "beating the Nazis" hook?

Could a Black woman performing in a different arena be more successful?

# CHAPTER TWO

## Broken Foot Composer: FLORENCE PRICE (1887-1953)

*To begin with I have two handicaps — those of sex and race."*

In 1939, celebrated soprano Marian Anderson was barred from performing at a Washington, DC venue because of her race. The group that owned Constitution Hall, the Daughters of the American Revolution (DAR), refused to let a Black woman perform for an integrated audience, but they did not foresee her triumph. The now historic concert moved instead to the Lincoln Memorial, after First Lady Eleanor Roosevelt intervened, and Anderson's "rich, vibrant contralto of intrinsic beauty" rang out to 75,000 people assembled there, with millions more listening by radio. The song Anderson chose as her finale: "My Soul's Been Anchored in the Lord," by composer Florence Price.

Ever heard of her?

## *From Little Rock to New England and Back*

Little Miss Smith performed her first recital at age 4 (her mother was her piano teacher) in Little Rock, Arkansas, and traveled with her mother in early childhood to England and France. As the daughter of an educated, activist Black family in Little Rock, she met distinguished guests, including Frederick Douglass. Florence was influenced and inspired by one of Little Rock's legendary African-American educators, Charlotte Andrews Stephens, who had dreams of becoming a composer but never did, instead working as an educator for 70 years!

Young Florence (not yet Price) passed as Mexican, at her mother's urging, when she entered the New England Conservatory of Music in Boston at age 16. She earned a double major in Organ Performance and Piano Pedagogy (the only student in her class to double-major).

After college, she worked as a music teacher and head of the music department at Clark University in Atlanta. She then returned to Little Rock, marrying lawyer Thomas Price in 1912. Two daughters, Florence Louise and Edith, were born to the couple; a stillborn son was memorialized by her song, "To My Little Son."

## *Break a Foot, Write a Symphony*

Price sampled African rhythms and folk melodies while composing in the classical tradition, and also set Langston Hughes' poems to music — most notably his "Songs to a Dark Virgin" cycle — which the Chicago Daily News in 1941 called "one of the greatest immediate successes ever won by an American song." Music critic Penelope Peters wrote of the piece:

"Hughes deliberately introduced ambiguity into his poem through the verbs 'hide' and 'annihilate.' Price captures that ambiguity by using an unstable tonic harmony throughout the accompaniment, including the tonic chord in the final cadence."

Price and her family were living in Chicago at the time, having moved there following the 1927 lynching of a Black man in Little Rock that terrorized the Black community thriving there. She ended the marriage to her abusive husband, attorney Thomas Price, and became a single mom with two kids.

Always a music teacher to make ends meet, she also composed advertising jingles for contests under a pseudonym to bring in some money. Meanwhile, Price waited in vain for the kind of success enjoyed by white contemporaries like the synthesizing American composer Aaron Copeland.

One of her few big breaks came (literally) when an injury laid her up long enough to compose the "romantic, large in its scope and richly textured" Symphony No. 1 in E Minor. That composition won the prestigious $500 Wanamaker Prize in 1932, but Price wrote to a friend,

"I found it possible to snatch a few precious days in the month of January in which to write undisturbed. **But, oh dear me, when shall I ever be so fortunate again as to break a foot!** [authors' emphasis]"

Major performers in classical music like Leontyne Price and Roland Hayes sang her compositions, and the Chicago Symphony Orchestra presented her *Symphony No. 1* in 1933, the first performance of a Black female composer's work by a major orchestra.

## *"A Black artist living within a white canon"*

Being a Black artist meant struggling with prejudice, but it also brought creative wealth. Price became friendly with operatic soloist Marian Anderson, as both belonged to the National Association of Negro Musicians. And Price wrote in a set of program notes for her *Symphony in E minor,* "It is intended to be Negroid in character and expression. In it no attempt, however, has been made to project Negro music solely in the purely traditional manner. None of the themes are adaptations or derivations of folk songs." In other program notes Price wrote:

> "In all types of Negro music, rhythm is of preeminent importance. In the dance, it is a compelling, onward-sweeping force that tolerates no interruption.... All phases of truly Negro activity — whether work or play, singing or praying — are more than apt to take on a rhythmic quality."

To quote from the *New York Times* tribute, "Welcoming a Black Female Composer into the Canon. Finally":

> "Marquese Carter, a doctoral student at Indiana University who specializes in Price's work, said in an interview that she 'uses the organizing material of spirituals. You may not hear direct quotation, but you will hear playing around with pentatonicism, playing around with call and response, some of these organizing principles that African-American scholars like Amiri Baraka have pointed out as indicative of Black musical discourse.'

"'Florence Price is a representation in music of what it means to be a Black artist living within a white canon and trying to work within the classical realm,' Mr. Carter added. 'How do we, through that, create a sound that sounds our culture, sounds our experience, sounds our embodied lives?'"

Over the course of her career Price created more than 300 works of art, and won many prizes.

## Recovering a "Treasure Trove"

Price's work is in revival now. The Albany label recently published two newly discovered Violin Concertos, part of a treasure trove of Price's musical manuscripts discovered in an abandoned summer home in St. Anne, Illinois, as detailed in a February 2018 *New Yorker* piece "The Rediscovery of Florence Price." (They are now archived at the University of Arkansas.)

The artistic director and conductor of the Women's Philharmonic in San Francisco, Apo Hsu, observed:

"Her orchestrations are lush and immense — bigger than Tchaikovsky. In the *Mississippi River Suite*, she has a wonderful way of using the orchestra to depict life along the river, using the influences of the juba dance rhythms and other sounds and colors to create a sense of tapping back to African roots."

The Women's Philharmonic (now disbanded) sought out compositions by women we deserve to hear.

"'We had a difficult time even locating her works,' says Hsu ... who learned that the scores for 'The

Oak' (c. 1934) and 'Mississippi River Suite' (c. 1934) were sitting on shelves in a library at the Eastman School of Music in Rochester, N.Y., and in a private collection at Yale University, untouched for decades.

"'We chose Florence Price because her music is wonderfully rich, she orchestrates really well and she's so well-versed in musical language. As an arranger of spirituals and songs, she had such a great reputation and created a great wealth of work, but when it came to her orchestral pieces, they were not being performed.'"

As the daughter of a dentist, Price had grown up and been educated in Little Rock's affluent professional class; by the time she was a single mom in Chicago, the structural discrimination against her gender and race had conspired to make her poor. At one point she had to resort to living with the family of her talented student, the composer Margaret Bonds. The two women composed together and inspired each other.

Alex Ross observed in *The New Yorker* profile, "not only did Price fail to enter the canon; a large quantity of her music came perilously close to obliteration. **That run-down house in St. Anne is a potent symbol of how a country can forget its cultural history**" [authors' emphasis].

The arts blog *J's Theater* quotes Marquese Carter on Price:

"Everything she was doing was musically mainstream but at the same time idiosyncratic. Her music has kind of a luminous quality that strikes me as her own.

Our understanding of American modernism of the 1930s and 1940s is not complete without Price's contribution."

## *Analysis*

Never heard of Florence Price? You're probably not a classical music performer or composer, but even if you are that's no guarantee you know of her fine work. As Price wrote to prominent Boston Symphony Orchestra conductor Serge Koussevitzky in 1943 (who never replied):

> "To begin with I have two handicaps – those of sex and race. I am a woman ... Unfortunately the work of a woman composer is preconceived by many to be light, froth, lacking in depth, logic and virility. Add to that the incident of race — I have Colored blood in my veins — and you will understand some of the difficulties that confront one in such a position ... I would like to be judged on merit alone."

Price clearly saw herself at the intersection of sexism and racism in the white male world of classical music. In addition to her self-described handicaps, how much did coping with and eventually leaving her abusive husband hold Price back from fame commensurate with her talent? And we wonder how much the economic burden of raising two children on her own hampered her ability to achieve her ambitions.

Maybe an affluent white artist unencumbered by a husband or dependents could have gotten the recognition she deserved?

# CHAPTER THREE

# Weary of Maestros:
# MICHAEL WEST (1908-1991)

*"I was obsessed with my own work."*

In 1908, a revolutionary artist was born in Ohio; she received the name Corinne Michelle West. With the privilege of inherited wealth, she was able to indulge her self-described mystic nature to pursue a life devoted to stoking her creative fire; without children to care for, she was able to become one of the most prolific and accomplished painters of the New York school of Abstract Expressionists. With a name that a friend told her sounded like "a debutante's daughter," she encountered many barriers to exhibiting her powerful avant-garde paintings, so in her twenties she changed her name to Michael West.

Ever heard of her?

## *"Creation is going beyond understanding"*

If you have, it is likely to have been in a mention that she was close friends — some say lovers, though West said not — and perhaps even the "muse" of the better known but less talented painter, Arshile Gorky.

Her explorations of Cubism probably remind you of another, more famous, Cubist practitioner; the comedienne Hannah Gadsby observed in her viral art rant that Picasso may have painted from multiple perspectives, but all of them excluded women. Cubism was the nursery of abstraction, the place where representation shattered and began moving in the direction of non-objective art, along with an impulse to activate the whole canvas.

West spent her early years studying piano and briefly was an actress who married her male lead, a union that lasted only a year. She soon found her true calling, traipsing to galleries for hours at a time, drinking in images until achieving "exhaustion … exhileration [sic]," and then returning to her studio to paint. She wrote in her journal, "Most artists have psychic abilities otherwise they cannot create. Creation is going beyond understanding and logic — to an esoteric field."

Art critic Dore Ashton observed in a 1999 essay for the posthumous exhibition "Automatic Paintings" that West had been strongly influenced by Surrealist poets and, later, by the calligraphy of Zen masters exhibited in 1958 at the Museum of Modern Art in New York.

## *"I have had enough of maestros"*

Miriam L. Smith on the website Art Resource Group wrote:

> "In 1946 West made reference in her writings
> to 'The New Art,' later known more formally

as Abstract Expressionism. West embraced
Abstract Expressionism, including the concept
of Action Painting, more closely than most of her
contemporaries."

In her twenties West was a student — along with many of
the big names in Abstract Expressionism — of the influential
teacher Hans Hoffman, whose "push/pull" theory of activating
the entire picture plane eventually came to dominate mid-20th
century American painting. West reportedly considered the
admirers who flocked around Hoffman to be something akin
to a cult, and she moved on in her own art education, saying of
Hoffman's bombastic style of teaching, "I have had enough of
maestros." According to Willette,

> "West apparently learned that she could work in
> large brushstrokes with a big paintbrush and keep
> the canvases to a large scale. She maintained the
> easel painting tradition … when one measures
> her canvases, one can see that they were sized
> to fit her body: the size of the brush her hand
> could hold, the distance her arm could travel
> from end to end, as she swept across the surface.
> The canvases were as tall as an average woman's
> height, minus a few inches and as wide as her
> outstretched arms."

West worked in multimedia before it was fashionable,
incorporating sand and other materials in her paintings, at
times pouring them on the canvas and moving them around
with a palette knife rather than using a brush. When Peggy
Guggenheim visited her studio in 1946, she said she was
impressed; yet, she never collected or exhibited West's work.
Gallery owner and West collector Stuart Friedman wonders,

"Was there room for only one Jackson Pollock in her stable? Were the works too wild and expressive for a woman?"

## *"The new art the new peace"*

On November 11, 1945 West was in her NYC studio.

> "As I write these words - a great parade of tanks and guns roar under my 5th Avenue window - the noise is deafening - hysterical - as the planes soar over head the birds soar - fly wildly about - some below some above the planes in the sky - it is a grey, cloudy, moody spring day - the feel of spring in the air is too soon - queer - it's a Cezanne. This glorious roar - this beautiful abstract scene of people lined all along the curb - looking up - at these guns pointed toward the sky - is the new poetry the new art the new peace - which for a moment - is actually seen and heard - like a great love never dying - the triumph of active mysticism realized - for a moment - good surpasses evil. Good conquers even in this world. Evil is too slow - as usual."

We can forgive West's optimism and naïveté about the fall of fascism from her vantage point in history; later, her work would reflect the disillusionment and grief of the impact of nuclear weapons dropped on Japan. A poem she wrote expressed the sense that would emerge in paintings like the altered cubist painting "Harlequin" (1946), and "Nihilism" (1949), compositions featuring obscuring blasts of silvery bright light bursting in their centers.

**"Rebel March 1948"**

Black Hands Crowd the Angry Dark

With Tales of Fire Coughing —

Money — genius —

unlimited or even limiter

What a ludicrous price —praying —

Dismantled — disarmed —

the artist in society —suffocates —

## *Left out of the Canon*

With a body of work so broad and accomplished, how did West get left out of the canon of Abstract Expressionists? She had a long career as a painter; in Rochester before moving to Manhattan she had several solo shows and also completed a commission of 14 panels for the set of a performance by the Ballet Petrouchka that must have been seen by many. Art historian Kristine Somerville notes,

> "While Abstract Expressionism took off and for decades was the 'house style,' its popularity didn't do enough to boost West's career. She received less press and fewer exhibitions than her male peers, though she eventually showed her work in Manhattan's prestigious Stable Gallery."

The deck was stacked against women and in favor of aggressive, hard-drinking, painters like Pollock who had visited West's studio with Guggenheim in 1946, and who acknowledged the influence of West's revolutionary painting style on his own work. (His wife, the talented Abstract

Expressionist painter Lenore "Lee" Krasner, often signed her paintings with a gender neutral L.K.) If the Cold War was all about who had the biggest nuclear missile, the celebrated painting of the New York School tended to be about who had the biggest ego writ large on the biggest canvas. Bars like Cedar Tavern in Greenwich Village, where the artists drank together and fought each other, were not female-friendly spaces.

Perhaps it was West's lack of existential doubt that made her creative persona difficult for hyper-masculine critics and artists to understand? As Ashton put it:

> "Her naive belief in the existence of some inner self stood her in good stead. While others wrestled with the dubious possibility that there could be an 'inner self' to which one must be true, West had no doubts. As a result rawness, even awkwardness, became a virtue ... She took seriously the general point of view among her peers that painting was a process, a way of living, a way of being, and not just a product ..."

## "Like a heroine in a historic novel"

In 1968, West published a portfolio of paintings and poems responding to the tragedy of the Vietnam War; *greenwich village and other poems* is now a rare collector's item. In 1970, West suffered a stroke but continued working as a painter despite that physical setback. She had now been divorced twice, never subordinating her own career to that of a husband. Detailing her reasons for declining Gorky's repeated proposals of marriage, she wrote,

> "There was no sex between Gorky & I - for 3 reasons - 1 - it was precluded by our feeling for art. 2 - I was getting over a divorce from an actor

- Randolph Nelson - Gorky from Marnie - we
felt destroyed by these painful experiences - one
does not forget - you carry your feelings with you
- cotinuely [sic] like a long trauma. (3rd Reason)
I thought he needed a Rich sophisticated person
who would give him 2 children and help manage
his career."

"Michael West's life spans American Abstract art like a
heroine in an historic novel in that she has left behind some
truly thrilling paintings," wrote Dore Ashton for West's
posthumous show at 123 Watts Gallery in NYC.

## *Analysis*

Educating her eye, immersing herself in the creative process,
showing her work, getting out to shows and rubbing elbows
with the male artists who eclipsed her — none of it was
enough. Avoiding the demands of mothering, privileged to
come from enough family wealth to be able to afford studio
space, materials and the time to paint — not enough either.
The disdain that critics and male artists of the 20th century
had for women blinded them to West's soaring talent. When
Abstract Expressionist promoter Clement Greenberg wrote
condescendingly of the artist Anne Truitt, "with the help of
monochrome the artist would have been able to dissemble her
feminine sensibility behind a more aggressively far-out, non-
art look," at least he was noticing her. West and her impressive
body of work never got a mention.

Maybe a woman among Communists with their creed of
gender equality could rise according to her talent?

# CHAPTER FOUR

# Defender of the Poor: EMMA TENAYUCA (1916-1999)

*"I was arrested many times. I didn't think in terms of fear, I thought in terms of justice."*

On a warm August night in 1939, Emma Tenayuca prepared to address a meeting of Communist Party members at San Antonio's Municipal Auditorium. She was one of the featured speakers based on her reputation as a successful labor organizer of cigar workers and pecan shellers, and now as chair of the Texas Communist Party. Tenayuca had seen hooded Ku Klux Klan marches as a child, and now the KKK was gathered outside with an anti-communist mob throwing bricks and stones and threatening to lynch her. Mayor Maury Maverick, who had given permission to use the auditorium in the face of fierce opposition, ended up spiriting Tenayuca and others away to safety via a hidden passageway under the building.

Ever heard of her?

If you're Tejana or a student of labor history you might have, but why do most of us know about Cesar Chavez and not his predecessor Emma Tenayuca?

## *"I was not listened to"*

The mob trashed the building that summer night in 1939 in what would be the biggest riot in San Antonio's history, with damage estimated at $5,000 (nearly $100,000 in today's dollars). Thirty-five hundred people then used the now vacated space to hold an impromptu meeting on "Americanism." Fleeing from a racist mob marked the end of San Antonio native Tenayuca's brilliant career as a human rights activist and labor organizer.

"I didn't want to hold the meeting, but I was not listened to," Tenayuca told a San Antonio Express-News reporter in 1990.

Prominent among those who didn't listen to Tenayuca was her husband at the time, Homer Brooks (né Baratsky):

> Tenayuca: "He was one of these inflexible Communists. He would not make an allowance for anything. He didn't have a sense of humor; my background was absolutely different from his ... some of the things that I considered humorous, well, he didn't even see it." (Laughter)

Tenayuca divorced Brooks in 1941, after three years of wedlock, and never remarried. Asked if she had any regrets about her activist days, she named only one: The riot effectively ended the political career of progressive Mayor Maverick.

Researcher Jerry Poyo questioned Tenayuca in 1987: "After the activities in '38, '39, did you make it a conscious decision to retire from labor organizing?" Her reply: "No, it was forced on me because I couldn't find jobs, so I left." The Federal Bureau of Investigation (FBI) was investigating her by 1939, and had infiltrators in Communist Party meetings informing on her.

She quit the Communist Party in 1939, disillusioned by the Soviet-Nazi non-aggression pact. But by 1941 the FBI had placed her name on a list for possible detention in the event of a national emergency. Although she advocated reform rather than revolution, Tenayuca was blacklisted in Texas.

## *An early start on political education*

Where did the organizer whom strikers called "la Pasionara" (translation: passion flower) get her fiery determination? First arrested in a labor action at age 16, Tenayuca told Poyo, "I was arrested a number of times. I didn't think in terms of fear — I thought in terms of justice." While other strikers faced violence, she said, "Perhaps I escaped any injury and so forth because I was quite young. I was a citizen." Motivated by a desire to "get them their rights" she got an early start on her political education by following her grandfather to the Plaza de Zacata in San Antonio.

> Tenayuca: "You could go to one corner of the plaza and listen to someone preaching and reading the Bible. You could go to another corner and hear someone reading the newspaper to a group of workers, reading the latest news from Mexico."

She would enjoy an ice cream cone while listening to diverse speakers.

Tenayuca indicated strong awareness of being bicultural, a Tejana who was both Texas-born and Hispanic. She noted the class distinction between her own community and that of immigrants from Mexico who came to Texas as laborers, and she organized in solidarity with the oppressed migrant workers. She was also aware of being biracial. Her mother's family, Zapedas descended from Spanish colonizers, did not fully accept her father's family, who were indigenous or Indios. The name Tenayuca is rare but closely resembles the name of a tribe of Native people who spell it a bit differently. Emma guessed that her surname's misspelling crept in as the result of an error when her grandmother had a group of cousins baptized en masse.

She often heard her family discuss politics while she was growing up, and she joined in. Tenayuca remembered her grandfather calling his sons to the house to consider whether or not to support Ma (Miriam Amanda) Ferguson for governor. Ferguson's husband had been impeached for stealing $75,000 from the University of Texas, but Ma Ferguson (who became the first woman governor of the Lone Star state) was running on a strong anti-KKK platform.

> Tenayuca: "So my grandfather rallied the entire Zapeda clan to vote for her … I remember I think I was about the third grade … I just told him, 'You're voting for the wife of a man who was impeached?'"

In later years Tenayuca identified some of her other influences:

> Tenayuca: "The woman for whom I had the greatest admiration was, of course, Elizabeth Gurley Flynn … I did have women heroes – Mrs. Roosevelt, Amelia Earhart, [athlete] Babe Didrikson. I clutched a dime and went down to see her play." (Laughter)

Flynn, a prominent labor organizer with the Wobblies (aka Industrial Workers of the World), also advocated for women's rights, including birth control and the right to vote. These cutting edge issues informed Tenayuca's political education in the early Twentieth Century.

## *Working Hard for the Workers*

Some of her many accomplishments before leaving Texas at age 25 include founding two chapters of the International Ladies' Garment Workers Union. She worked with the Women's International League for Peace & Freedom to feed striking pecan workers, poorly paid Mexican women whom she organized in probably her most famous campaign. Tenayuca helped in staging protests and letter-writing campaigns responding to the repatriation of Mexican-American activists by U.S. immigration officials. She was part of the effort to bring New Deal programs to San Antonio, which resulted in jobs for Spanish speakers.

In "*The Mexican Question in the Southwest*," which she co-authored with Brooks, she made common cause with another oppressed race: "This struggle [against housing and social services discrimination] must be joined with that of the Negro people." She also maintained of Hispanics, "We are not a conquered people."

She eventually relocated to San Francisco, California, where she returned to college, had a son, and began a long career teaching migrant workers' children.

## *Reflections on America*

Violent white men may have been able to drive her from a public political role, but Tenayuca never stopped reading and paying attention to politics. When a labor history researcher interviewed her for the Institute of Texan Cultures Oral History Collection at age 70, she had some incisive comments about current events.

> "I am disappointed by the intellectuals of America … We've been spending too much money on armaments. We haven't had any peace since World War II. We had troops in Korea, Vietnam, South American, Europe. We cannot continue to do that…

> "I was reading this morning's paper. Why covert actions? Why actually apply and make the policy of our country a terrorist under people such as [Colonel Oliver North] and Poindexter? … Some of the revelations are amazing.

> "[Of then President Reagan] He has almost, I would say, substituted covert actions for state diplomacy ... He's nothing but a bag of hot air.

> "Hollywood, you could have done better."
> (Laughter)

She made a rather dire prediction for the future, one that seems eerily prescient in the age of child refugees in cages at the Texas border, and the visibility of white nationalists who exhibit pride in racial hatred:

> "I have expected my country, your country, to become the scientific Athens, but I don't think that will be the case. They have been diverted into the same type of thing that Hitler was diverted to."

Speaking of the strikes she helped organize, Tenayuca reflected: "… it's the women who have led. And I just have a feeling, a very strong feeling, that if ever this world is civilized, that it would be more the work of women."

## *Analysis*

So, it looks like being a (woman) Communist didn't solve the silencing problem either. Tenayuca remained locally famous for some years. A civil rights organization in south Texas used to give awards for labor organizing in her name, but they were discontinued in 2015.

When she said she wasn't listened to about the meeting that produced the violent threats that drove her from Texas, who heard that? Maybe Tenayuca was born before her time. Maybe the future — a future with even more hostility toward Latinx migrant workers and refugees from political violence — will be ready to recognize women's leadership.

"[S]he was our passion, because she was our heart — defendiendo a los pobres, speaking out at a time when neither Mexicans nor women were expected to speak at all," said Carmen Tafolla, poet laureate, San Antonio, Texas.

# But That's All Behind Us Now, Right?

# CHAPTER FIVE

# Surveillance of Darkness: SIMONE BROWNE (b.1973)

*"Racism and anti-Blackness undergird and sustain the
intersecting surveillances of our present order."*

What do Beyoncé's sister Solange's hair, the song "Flash
Light" by the funk group Parliament, and so-called "lantern
laws" requiring Black slaves to carry a light after dark have in
common? All three illuminate the roots of modern surveillance
in racist practices against Black people, past and present. If
you're worried about Big Brother watching you, know that
Black people have been resisting and negotiating this threat
for much longer than most white people realize. "The body
made legible with the modern passport system has a history
in the technologies of tracking Blackness," wrote Professor
of Sociology Simone A. Browne at the University of Texas at
Austin, whose speciality is the racial history of surveillance.

Ever heard of her?

# *Racism in the Algorithm*

Much has been written lately about the structural racism of facial recognition search algorithms. Programmed primarily by white men, these technologies tend to render dark faces as either invisible, or miscategorized as non-human. In an ironic twist, dark eyes may not be accurately measured or identified by iris scanning technologies now in common use at airports. Browne calls our attention to what she describes as "security theater" performed by the Travel Security Administration (TSA).

Most of us know how quickly this veers into theater of the absurd but, for travelers of color like Solange Knowles, the absurdity is also intrusive and harassing. (*Sidenote: I have personally watched TSA confiscate a Black woman's unopened package of waffle mix at LAX this summer, because "it's a powder." A soccer coach, she was taking the mix in her carry-on bag in order to feed the team at her destination.*)

Knowles turned the unwelcome experience of having her hair probed by TSA into a game on Twitter, where she invited followers to guess "What did TSA find in Solange's Fro?" While admitting that, "I guess I could hide a joint up there," Knowles claimed "Discrim-FRO-nation" had targeted her for wearing an Afro-style wig. What is sometimes called "Black girl hair politics" occurs not only at airports, but also at work, where braids are deemed "unprofessional," and in schools, where girls are suspended for wearing their hair in a "wrong" style. It's almost as if the very fact of being a Black female is perceived as a threat in white-dominated spaces.

## *Marking, Branding, Illuminating Black Persons*

In a society built on the coerced labor of kidnapped Africans, a multitude of restrictions developed to contain the fear of slave owners and other whites. Browne points out that branding captives with hot irons was one of the more gruesome, and common, of these practices. Branding literally turned a slave's skin into a marker of their status as a commodity, claimed as the property of someone else — property that could be traced and recovered. In Browne's own words, "The historical formation of slavery is not outside of the historical formation of surveillance."

She discusses the observation, by David Lyons in Enemy of the State, that the U.S. "belief in the efficacy of technology 'solutions' far outstrips any evidence that technical devices can be relied upon to provide 'security.'" How did this belief grow and take root? Browne studied three movies (*Enemy of the State, Men in Black,* and *I, Robot*) starring actor Will Smith that provided, in her view, "product placement" for modern surveillance technologies. She observes how Smith's movies help sell surveillance gadgets as necessary, protective, and accurate when, in reality, they may be none of those things.

One of the chapters in Browne's book *Dark Matters: On the Surveillance of Blackness* takes its title from a line in Parliament's 1977 "Flash Light" song: "Everybody's got a little light under the sun." This chapter is where Browne discusses New York City's 18th century law requiring Black people to illuminate themselves at night. "Any white person was deputized to stop those who walked without the lit candle after dark. So you can see the legal framework for stop-and-frisk policing practices was established long before our contemporary era," Browne told interviewer Claudia Garcia-Rojas.

As Professor Imani Perry of the Princeton Center for African American Studies pointed out, "There's a long history of race and policing being deeply connected."

## *"Absented history"*

Shedding more light on her investigations into the security history of NYC, Browne said:

> "I was recently looking at the work of Marie Van Brittan Brown. Brown was a nurse living in Queens, New York, often working the night shift, and her husband, Albert Brown, was an electronics technician. In 1966, they developed blueprints for the first home security system — closed-circuit televisions, remote-control entry, intercoms, recording devices that could be accessed within a home — and in 1969, they got the patent.
>
> "So, this Black woman living in Queens and concerned with crime decided to do something about it. What does it mean for a Black woman to center her conditions at a time when the police response was quite lax?
>
> "The Browns were granted the patent in 1969, and this patent is cited by numerous patents up until this day, like video doorbells, which people now use, or you can use your smartphone app to see who's at your door and you can be someplace else.
>
> "That's a kind of absented history ..."

Browne is doing something valuable when she makes visible the history of modern surveillance. She also shows us the significance of "dark sousveillance," Black people using the tools of the modern security state to resist or escape incarceration, injury or death.

## *Art and Surveillance*

The insights of artists who comment on the modern surveillance state are also part of Browne's research focus. As she explains in *Dark Matters*:

> "… creative texts offer ways to understand [author bell hooks' terms] Black looks and talking back as oppositional practices that challenge the stereotyped representations of controlling images and their material effects. My use of [Robin] Rhode's *Pan's Opticon* (2008) and [Adrian] Piper's *What It Is, What It Isn't #3* (1991) is a way of drawing on Black creative practices in order to articulate a critique of the surveillance of Blackness."

*Pan's Opticon*, an art installation by South African artist Robin Rhode, is a reference to the 1791 Panopticon design discussed in *Dark Matters*, a plan created by two Englishmen to effect total surveillance of incarcerated people. As such, it is a chilling precursor of a U.S. total surveillance system already in place. All emails, text messages, mobile phone calls, financial records, health records and anything else digitized are readily available to the federal government via back channels provided by Google, Facebook and other platforms. It also hints at the current U.S. prison system, the largest on the planet, with a population 40% Black when Black people constitute only 13% of people in the country.

# Cyberfeminists, Target Customers and Separated Families

In 2014 Browne participated in Deep Lab, "a congress of cyberfeminist researchers, organized ... to examine how the themes of privacy, security, surveillance, anonymity, and large-scale data aggregation are problematized in the arts, culture and society." Deep Lab members worked together in a "book sprint" and published their collaboration intended to "exploit the potential for creative inquiry lying dormant in the deep web." This work is on the cutting edge of human life as shaped by interactions with digital technology. One of the chapters in *The Book* which resulted from Deep Lab's 2014 collaboration, "Commodifying Life" by Jen Lowe, focused on the cybersecurity of the unborn:

> "... statisticians like Andrew Pole at Target ... used data mining to come up with an algorithm to determine not only if a female customer was pregnant, but how far along her pregnancy was, so Target could send coupons timed to very specific stages of her pregnancy ...
>
> "A pregnant woman's marketing data is worth 15 times an average person's data."

Browne participates in some interesting groups. She serves on the Executive Board of HASTAC, an "academic social network" that is open to anyone who cares to participate, with a focus on the humanities in a technology-driven age. Recently HASTAC supported "a design sprint and hackathon" held at the Digital Humanities 2018 conference in Mexico City. People responding to the crisis of deliberate separation of families at the U.S.-Mexico border came together to work with data on ICE detentions, which had been aggregated in advance by the group Torn Apart / Separados. Project ideas that emerged included outreach to academia and media, data visualizations that could help immigration lawyers, and investigating what role U.S. military bases play in immigration control. The effort continues to be crowdsourced, with online structures in place to welcome new collaborators.

## "Machine reading of emotions"

Information technology is a tool that can be used for good or evil, and Browne wants people to notice the human attitudes invisibly embedded in technologies of control:

> "You have a large push into affective computing technologies, the kind of machine reading of emotions being used at airports, for example, in Israel, which monitor people for blood pressure, for sweat and for changes in their voice, and then assign a threat category or score to them. These kinds of affective computing technologies amp up the role of affect, which, as we know, is something that is socially constructed.

> "This gets us to think about: Who gets marked as 'angry' prior to any reaction? ... This harkens back to the controlling images of the 'angry Black woman' and the 'threatening Black man.'"

Browne works skillfully, as a well-liked university professor, a presenter at conferences and an academic journal editor, to make visible to many people the connections among different kinds of surveillance:

> "Recently it seems, at least in the U.S., the relationship between surveillance as understood

by the PATRIOT Act or [Edward] Snowden's
revelations of warrantless wiretapping is,
for many people, becoming understood as
existing alongside with the Black Lives Matter
movement's call to 'stop killing us,' mass
incarceration, and whether or not the police
should wear bodycams.

"Right now what I find the most scary is the trust
people have in corporations that they don't have
in each other. The amount of data and personal
information we hand to them everyday which
people don't question scares me."

It may be the 21st century, but a woman of color working in
academia still faces the same old barriers as she did in the 20th
century. A 2016 study by the National Center for Education
Statistics found 55% of tenured professors in the U.S. were
white males, and another 27% were white females. Only 2% are
Black women. But is being a college professor who's an expert
in her field — even in a cutting edge field like surveillance —
a path to fame? I don't know, maybe ask Carl Sagan or Neil
deGrasse Tyson. Or maybe Professor Browne just isn't old
enough yet for her name to be generally known. Maybe it takes
a Black woman a whole lifetime of outstanding work in her field
to break through into public consciousness.

Surveillance of Darkness: SIMONE BROWNE (b.1973)

# 6

# CHAPTER SIX

# Dissent Is Patriotic:
# ANN WRIGHT (b.1947)

*"Citizens have a responsibility to take action when they see crimes being committed."*

It was March 20, 2011 when retired U.S. Army Colonel Ann Wright was arrested outside Quantico Marine Base in Virginia. Iraq war crimes whistleblower Chelsea Manning, a transsexual born as Bradley, was being detained in abusive conditions — solitary, sleep deprivation, forced nudity. While Manning endured hell inside Quantico, Wright stood with Manning's supporters outside facing roughly 60 military police, state police, town police, county sherrifs, mounted police, K-9 police, riot squad police, and commandos in camouflage armed with automatic weapons. Wright and others were protesting peacefully when officers chose to shut down the major road that they were standing alongside, "kettling" the protesters into the road using metal barricades (*Note: I write here from personal experience. I was there.*) In an act of civil disobedience, Wright sat down in the road. Vietnam War whistleblower Daniel Ellsberg and several others were inspired to sit down with her. The last Wright was seen that day, she was objecting as riot police wrenched her arm because she did not get up quickly enough when being arrested.

Ever heard of her?

## *The Making of a World Traveler*

As a girl growing up in Arkansas in the 1950s and '60s, Mary Annette Wright (now just "Ann" Wright) wanted wider horizons:

> Wright: "I was a Girl Scout. The Girl Scouts in the late 1950s had some programs where young women in The South could travel and meet other girls: Natchez to New Orleans, for example, and hiking in the Smoky Mountains, and going to the Girl Scout Roundup in Idaho. That kind of laid the groundwork for me wanting to travel the world."

That same desire to live outside of the restrictions of what was expected of young women of the time led her to join the U.S. Army as a Second Lieutenant immediately upon graduating from the University of Arkansas in 1967.

> Wright: "It wasn't that I wanted to go kill anyone, or was in favor of the war in Vietnam. I was being trained [in college] to be a teacher, and I didn't want to be a teacher. Or I could have been a nurse, and I didn't want to be a nurse, or a secretary, and I didn't want to be a secretary, or a homemaker, and I didn't want to be a homemaker. [The recruiter promised her she would be able to travel, and as a non-nurse, she would not go to Vietnam.] At that time, having

served for two years active duty made a veteran eligible for four years for trades training or college. I rationalized it in my own mind that I was not going to kill anyone.

"I used part of my GI Bill for pilot training — commercial instrumentation training — and part for graduate school [the U.S. Naval War College] and law school [University of Arkansas]. The GI Bill's [benefits] are nothing now compared to that. Instead, there are these huge [cash] signing bonuses."

## *An Officer and a Dissenter*

Wright entered the U.S. military less than a decade before a major transition to the integration of women into the armed forces. The Army disbanded the Women's Army Corps (The "WACs") in 1978. In the late 1960s when young Lieutenant Wright began her military service, women were fewer than 1% of the armed forces, and there was a quota limiting their numbers. (As of 2018, women are 16% of enlisted troops, and 18% of the officer corps.)

Women officers were having to catch up with men who had been in the Army for 10 years. It was a difficult transition.

Wright: "I helped form 'Women in the Army Group' on many [military] bases and at West Point. Enlisted or official women could come to lunches and take part in discussion of challenges, such as harassment. It was considered to be a challenge to the chain of command — what were those women talking about?! I would bring issues to the commanding officer, such as lack of career advancement."

The Army developed a program, Direct Combat Probability Coding (DCPC), describing how far forward each unit would be on a European battlefield, based on war games. Some women in the Army, including officers, were ejected from their units even though they had served in them successfully for a long time.

> Wright: "In 1982, I went to DC on another pretext to bring [the issue of military women being ejected] to the attention of Assistant Secretary of Defense Larry Korb, who was speaking at a conference. And as he was talking about opportunities for women, I stood up in the balcony [of the auditorium] and yelled, 'That's not true! Women in the Army are being kicked out of their units!' Korb stopped and said, 'What did you say?!' I repeated it. Korb demanded of the big brass sitting in the front row, 'Is this true?' Then there was a big brou-haha."

The Army stopped the coding of these units because of Wright's intervention.

This incident prefigures the many times she, along with other peace activists, interrupted congressional hearings to protest the Iraq War, the military use of torture, and U.S. foreign policy after September 11.

Another organization Wright worked with was the Defense Advisory Committee on Women in the Services, composed of civilian women and men appointed by the Secretary of Defense as advisors on the recruitment and retention of women in the military. She also wrote for *Minerva: Journal of Women and War*, a peer-reviewed scholarly magazine publishing articles on women's military history, and the ways armed conflict affects women.

## *From Colonel to Diplomat*

Wright made a major career transition in the mid-1980s when she left the Army join the foreign service:

> Wright: "I decided to move from the Army in 1985 when I had applied to go into the military attache program [overseas]. Their job is to coordinate with the military of the host country. I had worked in Panama with the militaries of Central and South America. I had been to many of the embassies in Latin America, and I kinda like how [embassy personnel] live. You don't have to get up so darn early in the morning!
>
> "The Army said, 'You can't do that - women can't be military attaches.'"

Wright challenged this decision, all the way up the chain of command to a 4-star Army general who had never noticed that no women served as military attaches, but after her drawing it to his notice, thought that women should be able to serve in this capacity. However, the Head of Defense Intelligence Agency (DIA) thought otherwise and kept the policy.

> Wright: "I had taken the foreign service exam several years before, and had received an offer from the State Department previously. I went from being a Colonel in the Army to start at the lowest level at the State Dept."

While working as a diplomat in numerous countries in Central Asia, including Afghanistan and Mongolia, Sierra Leone, Micronesia, Grenada and Nicaragua, Wright continued her service in the Army Reserves, finally retiring in 1996.

Highlights of her successful diplomatic career include helping to open the U.S. embassy in Uzbekistan, and re-opening the embassy in Kabul in 2001. Perhaps the most rewarding moment of her diplomatic career was receiving the State Department's Award for Heroism as Charge d'Affaires during the evacuation of Sierra Leone in 1997.

## *Good-bye State Department. Hello, Peace Movement!*

In early 2003, as an international movement was roaring its opposition to the United States' threat to bomb and invade Iraq, Wright was serving as deputy chief of mission, this time in Ulaanbaatar, Mongolia. Remote from the waving banners in the immense antiwar marches from Italy to California, the seasoned diplomat wrote a letter to her boss, Secretary of State Colin Powell. She finally sent it five weeks after writing it, as the American assault on Baghdad began. The letter read in part:

> "This is the only time in my many years serving America that I have felt I cannot represent the policies of an Administration of the United States. I disagree with the Administration's policies on Iraq, the Israeli-Palestinian conflict, North Korea and curtailment of civil liberties in the U.S. itself. I believe the Administration's policies are making the world a more dangerous, not a safer, place. I feel obligated morally and professionally to set out my very deep and firm concerns on these policies and to resign from government service as I cannot defend or implement them."

As has now been well-documented, the U.S. war of aggression against Iraq did not meet the two criteria for legal war as established by the United Nations: defense against an immediate, credible threat; and/or the approval of the United Nations Security Council (UNSC). Wright warned the Secretary of State that:

> "I believe we should not use U.S. military force without UNSC agreement to ensure compliance. In our press for military action now, we have created deep chasms in the international community and in important international organizations. Our policies have alienated many of our allies and created ill will in much of the world."

In addition to Wright's principled and deeply felt opposition to the U.S. war on Iraq, a country weakened by 13 years of sanctions, she also spoke of her opposition to "the Administration's lack of effort in resolving the Israeli-Palestinian conflict, including "our considerable financial influence on the Israelis to stop destroying cities and on the Palestinians to curb its youth suicide bombers." She objected to the Bush Administration's "lack of substantive discussion, dialogue and engagement over the last two years" with nuclear-armed North Korea. And finally, Wright declared her refusal to support "the Administration's unnecessary curtailment of civil rights following September 11."

As a person trained in the law, Wright argued, "[s]olitary confinement without access to legal counsel cuts the heart out of the legal foundation on which our country stands" at Guantanamo and the U.S. "black sites" of imprisonment and torture elsewhere in the world. Wright ended her letter on a heartfelt note: "I hate to leave the Foreign Service, and I wish you and our colleagues well."

With that, Wright returned, after decades of service abroad, to her own country. Mulling over how her career in the State

Department was an unplanned preparation for her third career as a citizen diplomat and peacemaker, Wright remembered:

> "I knew more people who were dissidents in their home countries than in the United States. I lived most of my adult life outside the United States. I was not involved in any peace organizations, or actually challenging U.S. government policies. It was almost like coming into a new country [the anti-war/pro-peace movement] and I was approaching it like a diplomat in a foreign country, analyzing, talking to lots of people, trying to figure out what's going on.

> "I didn't know any people in the U.S. peace movement when I resigned in 2003. In the summer of 2003, a group in Washington got in touch about testifying at an informal hearing in the Senate. That was the first time that I met the other two people who resigned from the State Department in opposition to the U.S. war on Iraq [Brady Kiesling, Chief of the economics section at the U.S. Embassy in Athens, Greece, and John Brown, who was on a special assignment at Georgetown University, a specialist in Russian affairs].

> "In 2004, I happened to be in Santa Barbara, and I saw these crosses out on the beach, and asked this person what it was all about. ['Arlington West' commemorated the dead, both Iraqi and American, in the Iraq War]. I'll never forget him. Lane Anderson [a member of Veterans for Peace] said, 'Well, hell, you're one of us! Why don't you come to our national convention in Boston and meet all these other people? You need to know about us, and we need to know about you!'"

So, with that warm invitation Wright attended the 2004
Veterans For Peace convention in Boston, where she met
Medea Benjamin and Gael Murphy, CodePink co-founders.
Immediately following the VFP annual gathering, she attended
the huge raucous protests of the Iraq War at the Republican
National Convention in New York City. Wright recalled,
"Medea [at the VFP convention] said: 'You should come!' It
was fun ... it was amazing."

## Ending the Iraq War — for 8 Years

That engagement with the peace movement led to Wright's
deeper involvement the following summer, also following the
annual VFP convention in Dallas. In summer 2005, Wright
helped organize Camp Casey, an occupation of land near
President Bush's ranch in Texas initiated by bereaved, enraged
Gold Star Mother Cindy Sheehan. After losing her son Casey
in the Iraq War, Sheehan began camping out with the demand
that Bush explain what "noble cause" Casey had died for. Many
supporters, eventually up to 2,000, including recent returning
combat veterans, followed Sheehan, with Wright taking on
logistical responsibilities.

Her commitment to ending the war in Iraq was long-lasting.
Following her stint at Camp Casey, Wright co-authored
*Dissent: Voices of Conscience: Government Insiders Speak Out
Against the War in Iraq*, published in 2007. According to the
social media platform Goodreads, she and "coauthor Susan
Dixon tell the stories of government insiders and active-duty
military who have spoken out, resigned, leaked documents, and
refused deployment to bring attention to government lies and
actions they felt were illegal."

Wright participated with CodePink and other peace activists
in many disruptions of congressional hearings on the progress,

or lack of it, in the eight-year war that claimed the lives of up to one million Iraqis and thousands of Americans. She was arrested numerous times in direct actions to protest the war. (*Janet Weil, who wrote this book's introduction, had the honor of being arrested with Wright on the Golden Gate Bridge on New Year's Day, 2007, as we attempted to solemnly commemorate the 3,000th official American death in Iraq.*) She was also vocal in support of Lt. Ehren Watada, the only U.S. military officer to resign his commission and refuse to be deployed to Iraq.

Wright testified at the The People's Tribunal on the Iraq War in December 2016:

> "It is so important that after 13 years of war that Iraq has endured, after 15 years of war that Afghanistan has endured, that we remind ourselves of what has happened, and then we look at other places in the world ... that the war-mongering policies of our government and other governments that are creating crises around the world ... We must look at our history."

Wright's peace work has taken her to many places, but following the points in her resignation letter, she has focused most on the Israel-Palestine conflict, on the Korean peninsula, and on human rights violations committed by the use of drones in warfare.

## *Going to Gaza*

Wright has been on seven humanitarian relief missions to Gaza, at times having her laptop and phone confiscated amid violence by Israeli commandos boarding the boats in international waters. The most dangerous of the Gaza trips included the infamous Israeli attack on the Mavi Marmara in 2010; 10 of the relief workers on that boat were killed by Israeli armed forces, while Wright was arrested from another boat in the flotilla.

One of the boats in a 2011 flotilla effort expressed a theme central to Wright's life of public service: *The Audacity of Hope*. Her most recent Gaza relief mission was in July-August, 2018, a journey Wright described as intended

> "... to remind Europe of the inhuman exposure of the Israeli occupation and the situation on Gaza Strip. We have been on rivers and canals through Germany, Holland, Belgium and France. Many have taken note of our message and we have in most cases got the thumbs up. We have had meetings with Palestine activists mainly in Amsterdam, Rotterdam, Paris suburbs, Lyon, Avignon and Marseille."

In October, 2016 Wright was again illegally detained and jailed along with many others, including Nobel Peace laureate Mairead Maguire, while on the *Women's Boat to Gaza*. Wright explained in an interview in 2016:

> "I felt it was important to put my voice and my body where it counted and to be a part of an international group to challenge the Israeli naval blockade of Gaza."

After being released from jail and deported from Israel on October 6, 2016, Wright joined water protectors at Standing Rock to oppose the North Dakota Access Pipeline. She went on a speaking tour in Maine sharing her observations from those events, "Never Silent Until Our Sisters Are Free." She conducted a similar speaking tour in her home state of Hawai'i in 2011, where she has also been active in resisting the expansion of military bases and the pollution caused by existing bases.

A prolific writer, Wright published an account of police violence against unarmed protestors and the arrest of 141 water protectors, "At Standing Rock, A Native American Woman Elder Says 'This is What I Have Been Waiting for My Entire Life'" (Common Dreams, Nov. 8, 2016).

## *Women Crossing the DMZ in Korea*

In May 2015, Wright joined an international women's peace delegation, organized by activist-scholar Christine Ahn, to march across the demilitarized zone between North Korea and South Korea. The goals of the group Women Cross DMZ were ending the Korean War with a peace treaty, reuniting divided families, and ensuring that women be involved at all levels of the peace-building process. (The Korean War ended with a cease-fire and partition in 1953, and no peace treaty between North Korea and the United States has yet been negotiated.)

Prior to this high-visibility trip to both Koreas, Wright had been an active participant in the resistance by villagers on Jeju Island, South Korea, to the construction of a huge naval base that entombed the coral reefs of their traditional fishing grounds in concrete so U.S. warships could dock there.

She participated in a second International Peace Conference convened by the YMCA South Korea and held in Pyongyang, North Korea in summer 2018 as relations between two countries began to thaw. Wright called for an end to the travel ban and the opening of "interest sections" (a step toward embassies) in Pyongyang and Washington. As she explained in a Guardian article, "Direct interactions with North Koreans help humanize the American people in a country that has been so isolated from the west."

## *"To challenge the assassin drones"*

In November 2011, Wright faced trial in Syracuse, New York, as one of 38 protesters arrested at the New York Air National Guard base at Hancock Field. They were protesting the use of flying killer robots, specifically MQ-9 Reaper drones, which the 174th Fighter Wing of the Guard was remotely flying over Afghanistan. The drones killed many civilians — people the Pentagon referred to as "collateral damage" and the drone operators themselves sometimes called "bug splat" in reference to their appearance on the monitor screen in Syracuse.

Wright was among those who used white cloth splattered with red paint to stage a "die-in" at the main entrance to the base, which the protesters described as an act of nonviolent civil disobedience aimed at visualizing killing of civilians in both Afghanistan and Pakistan. At her trial, Wright was found guilty of trespassing, fined, and (ironically) sentenced to community service. She explained her motivation:

> "Citizens have a responsibility to take action when they see crimes being committed.
>
> "And this goes back to World War II, when German government officials knew what other parts of the German government were doing in executing six million Jews in Germany and other places, and that they took no action ... and they were held responsible later, through the Nuremberg trials.
>
> "And that is the theory on which we are acting, that we see that our government is committing crimes by the use of these drones, and that we, as citizens, have the responsibility to act."

Shut Down Creech is a recurring protest at Creech Air Force Base near Las Vegas with similar aims; Wright was there on March 6, 2015, in an attempt to block the main entrance to Creech, another drone remote control center. She explained that she was there along with dozens of other protesters...

> "... to challenge the assassin drones that are being operated from here to Afghanistan, Yemen and Pakistan ...
>
> "The statistics that we have, which have been done primarily by the Bureau of Investigative Journalism out of the UK, is that 95% of the people that are being killed — which is well over 5,000 people now — have been innocent civilians."

About 150 people, including members of Veterans for Peace, mobilized with Wright in the Nevada desert on that occasion.

## *Speaking Out Against the U.S. Empire*

By December 2015, Wright was in Okinawa supporting the local resistance to U.S. military bases located there. In a speech to a symposium there, she used strong words to condemn U.S. foreign policy, and she connected the Okinawa islanders' struggle to an infamous base and prison halfway around the world:

> "Let me assure you, we in the United States continue our struggle demanding a trial for all prisoners, the closing of the prison in Guantanamo and the return of the land to the people of Cuba. The U.S. military base is of no strategic importance to the United States, but instead is used as the symbol of U.S. imperialism

to the revolution of Cuba and the U.S. attempts over the past 60 years to overthrow the revolution."

"Over the past 100 years, Cuba, Nicaragua, El Salvador, Guatemala, Honduras, Grenada, Haiti, Germany, Italy, Spain, the Netherlands, Japan, Korea, the Philippines, Afghanistan, Iraq, Iran, Pakistan, Bahrain, Kuwait, Qatar, Saudi Arabia, Libya, Somalia, Djibouti, Diego Garcia have had the presence of U.S. military in their countries.

"Today, the United States empire has over 800 U.S. military installations around the world."

Wright has contributed numerous articles for online publications over the years including *Consortium News*, *Counterpunch*, *Alternet* and *Common Dreams*. She has been interviewed by Amy Goodman's TV show *Democracy Now!*, the national radio show "Flashpoints" and *The Guardian* in the U.K.

Her 2018 article, "How Military Operations in Somalia 25 Years Ago Influence Operations in Afghanistan, Iraq, Syria and Yemen Today," explains that, "The Law of Land Warfare and the Geneva Conventions are routinely violated in Afghanistan, Iraq, Syria and Yemen." The evolution — or devolution — of U.S. military tactics in the never-ending "War on Terror" leads to the grim likelihood of blowback at U.S. embassies and other facilities in foreign countries.

Wright translated the autobiography *I, Rigoberta Menchu: An Indian Woman in Guatemala* from the original Spanish in 1985. Rigoberta Menchú Tum, a K'iche' activist who has dedicated her life to publicizing the rights of Guatemala's indigenous feminists and promoting indigenous rights in the country, received the Nobel Peace Prize in 1992.

As this is being written amid warmongering from the federal government threatening Iran, it is hard not to be reminded of something Wright said in 2015 on Okinawa: "The United States has built permanent base infrastructure in every Persian Gulf country except one: Iran." No big surprise, then, that Iran is now a target of sanctions and bellicose threats.

## *Analysis*

Wright considers her lack of success in breaking the de facto mainstream media blackout of her and fellow/sister antiwar activists:

> Wright: "If you look at all of us who have been challenging the government (Medea Benjamin, Ray McGovern, etc.), we can get on RT, but we cannot get on MSNBC or other mainstream media. An exception was, Medea and I actually got on Fox a lot [during the Iraq War]. Once Bill O'Reilly turned off my mic because he didn't like what I was saying.

> "We [Ann and other dissidents] are never contacted about being on cable network news. I would say it's a blackout, not just as individuals, but voices of dissent against our government's policies.

> "Medea has broken into C-SPAN a little bit. [Korea expert] Christine Ahn has, actually in the last year and a half, gotten into some mainstream media that none of us have been able to. Because of Korea peace negotiations with Kim Jong-Un, Moon and Trump being such a big deal. Christine Ahn has not gotten arrested, she has chosen a path that she is known more as a policy analyst and not as a protester.

"My decision was to get arrested and be in these confrontational situations. We are seen as fringe people, who are not really foreign policy experts, although we have very strong backgrounds [in foreign affairs]. This lessens our opportunity to be on mainstream media. I have recognized that for years. I think it's important to have people make an example. It encourages other people to take more courageous actions, not necessarily that you have to be arrested, but to put yourself forward. No one else as a former army officer and diplomat is doing that — I think I'm the only one."

Wright's life is lived as an example of her belief, expressed in *Dissent*, "All actions have consequences, and nations, like individuals, are ultimately accountable for their actions."

So, how come you never see Ann Wright on television? Either as an empaneled expert with other foreign policy wonks, or in action doing historic things likes crossing the DMZ with Korean women from both sides of the cease-fire line? The same talking heads get mainstream media attention in the U.S. for foreign policy, wars and peace activism. Almost like there is a club for corporate media workers that has a very short vetted list of "experts" that can be counted on to toe the two party line, and not rock the boat of the status quo.

Even before she resigned from government service to become a full time dissenter, Wright was probably out of the running; when's the last time you saw a female military officer providing news commentary on very male topics like violent conflict? Maybe a woman who's an expert on, say, women would have a better shot at breaking through.

# CHAPTER SEVEN

# Where the Women Are: JONI SEAGER (b.1954)

*"Disaster is seldom gender neutral."*

In September, 2005, a well-known performer remarked on national television coverage of Hurricane Katrina: "George Bush doesn't care about black people." A few days later, feminist geographer Joni Seager took this infamous observation a giant step further in "Noticing Gender (Or Not) In Disasters." Writing on the website ScienceDirect.com, Seager noted:

> "By about the third day, reporters (mostly white) started to say out loud how noticeable it was that the people trapped in the disaster in New Orleans were mostly, undeniably, Black ... this enlightened 'noticing' by the media produced a moment of genuine inquiry as mainstream reporters and analysts started asking tough, targeted questions

about why this disaster fell so hard on one side of the race line."

Then Seager enriched this line of inquiry by making it intersectional. Noting that most of the casualties of Katrina were women — and that corporate media showed little interest in this fact, possibly because black women tend to be overlooked by the mainstream male gaze — she pointed out an ugly, unexamined truth:

> "[T]he lack of curiosity about the rapes in the midst of the New Orleans disaster is just one particularly disturbing aspect of this willful ignorance. Rapes have been reported by dozens of survivors, and mentioned as a subtext in several news stories but always in passing and with no follow-through: to date, there have been no attempts to verify the dozens of reports, no interviews with police chiefs about the magnitude of rape, no curiosity about the construction of masculinity that contemplates rape in conditions of such extreme human suffering, no disaster experts assuring us that rape-support teams are included in the rescue teams, no discussion about the medical and psychological resources that women will need who have survived unimaginable tragedy and stress **and have then also been raped** [emphasis is the author's]."

Ever heard of her?

So goes the life work of Joni Seager, Global Studies Professor at Bentley University and Consultant to the United Nations Environmental Programme: noticing what goes unnoticed by mainstream journalists, historians and other academics. In

1997 she acknowledged her debt to "the countless feminists
— most unnamed and unrecognized — who ... have been the
only ones insisting that it is important to ask questions about
where the women are." In her 1992 essay, "Women Deserve
Spatial Consideration," she wrote,

> "As an undergraduate Geography major at the
> University of Toronto in the early 1970s, I never
> once heard a classroom discussion of the role of
> women in the world, not even in the two-year-
> long Population Geography courses that I took
> — which, in retrospect, is an amazing feat ..."

## *An Atlas That Shows Women*

In her first *The State of Women in the World Atlas*, Seager
compiled and displayed data on the gender that was being
ignored in books with titles she cited as "early warning of the
extent to which the existence of women on earth was denied ...
*Plants, Man and Life*, *The Man-Made Environment*, and *Man's
Role in Changing the Face of the Earth*."

Visualizations using computer-generated images from
demographic data are commonplace now, but they were just
coming into their own when Seager's unique book came out
in 1986. In what might be considered a feminist geographer's
manifesto she wrote,

> "... global generalizations must not be used to
> mask the very real differences that exist among
> women country by country, region by region. It
> is through mapping that I believe we may best be
> able to strike a balance between the demands of
> representing both commonality and difference; at
> its best, mapping can simultaneously illuminate
> both."

In the introduction to the 4th edition in 1997, Seager identified some of the changes that had occurred for the women of the world over a decade:

> "On a positive note, there have been broad improvements in the conditions of daily life for many of the world's women. Women's and girls' education rates have shown considerable improvement, as have literacy rates ... most of the world's governments are now committed (at least on paper) to women's equality and to improving the status of women ...
>
> "However ... many women have experienced an absolute decline in the quality of their life ... The globalizing new world economy is based largely on exploiting 'flexible' markets of underpaid workers; women's participation as workers in this new world economy is not an unalloyed sign of progress ... women remain the poorest of the poor, everywhere."

For women and the children they nurture, this sad reality has remained unchanged through subsequent new editions. *The Penguin Atlas of Women in the World* (4th edition) was completely revised and updated for 2009, with maps displaying global data on access to contraception, maternal mortality rates, and the incidence of breast cancer. "Son Preference" is another way of looking at the status of girls, and Seager does so with maps titled "Unnatural selection," accompanied by graphs of nations that are "Choosing sons" while "Endangering daughters."

The explanatory note for the Beauty section of "Part Four: Body Politics" reads, "International beauty contests promote and export a white, Western standard of beauty. Globalization is accelerating the adoption of these standards around the world."

If information is power, Seager's series of atlases empower us in ways that could benefit everyone, because "to improve the state of women is to improve the state of the world." Microloan programs and other aid projects recognize that boosting women's economic well-being is an effective strategy to improving the lot of infants, children and men as well. Taking data that could be dry and making it compelling with "creative visualizations," Seager's atlases have been called "page turners" by critics. A typical comment by a satisfied customer: "Had to order this book for a class, and I love it more than I expected! Everyone should have one" (Kelsey Monaghan).

## *Lesbians in Love and at Work*

"Lesbian organizing has come out of the closet," noted Seager, chronicling changes for women in 1997. The freedom to love whom one chooses is represented in global mapping of "Lesbian Rights." It's a personal issue for Seager. Spouse Cynthia Enloe, also an academic researcher, has contributed much to Seager's work, especially in terms of perspective. Enloe's interest in using a gendered lens to uncover truths obscured by a focus on male experience came about when she ...

> "... spoke with a colleague at Clark [University], the only man on the faculty who was a veteran, about his experiences during the Vietnam war. He mentioned that Vietnamese women were hired by American soldiers to do their laundry. She began to wonder how history would be different if the entire war had been told through the eyes of these Vietnamese women."

Enloe and Seager have supported one another's thinking and research while focusing on militarism on the one hand, and geography on the other. In her book *The Big Push*, Enloe wrote, "It has been Joni with whom I have continued to investigate the twists and turns of modernizing patriarchy. Shared laughter, irreverence, energy, curiosity, companionship -- that's what a sustainable feminist partnership looks like."

As a wife-and-wife team they co-authored *The Real State of America Atlas: Mapping the Myths and Truths of the United States* (2011), a book that buyer Kris Kauffold said, "sits in my living room, and everyone seems to pick it up. Once they open it, they are hooked." The introduction reads, "Americans have been buoyed and burdened by myths since the continent's settlement." One of the first myths they take on is the alleged absence of Native people — a map of "Indian Country" precedes one of "American Empire." In some ways, it is a prescient book: "Turning Native Americans Into Someone Else's Logo" is a sidebar addressing the "deeply offensive" sports mascots, cartoons and practices that are so controversial today.

Seager's idea that "large corporations dominate the lives of Americans from birth to death" preceded the Occupy Wall Street anti-corporate movement that broke out in October 2011. Her close look at security fences and flying surveillance drones on the Mexico-U.S. border preceded the 2018 attempt to shut down migration by separating children from parents in families seeking asylum.

In 1995, Seager published *The State of the Environment Atlas: The International Visual Survey*, to present complex environmental information succinctly and powerfully. This atlas has had two editions thus far.

## *"My 2 degrees rant"*

Seager is not afraid of being controversial. A popular university professor, with a reputation for lively and engaging lectures, she has taken on the holy cow of climate change goals in articles and talks. Delivering the keynote "Feminism and Climate Change" at The Scholar & Feminist Conference 2010 at Barnard College, Seager gave what she calls "my 2 degrees rant." In response to world leaders identifying a 2 degree Celsius rise in global temperature as acceptable, Seager began to investigate where this metric had come from and what was the thinking behind it. What she found wasn't pretty.

> Seager: "At 1 degree of warming we have ... increasing malaria, extreme weather events ... glacial melts, droughts, floods, permafrost instability ...
>
> "So 2 degrees is not a very salubrious target ... 50% crop failures ... severe water shortages, perhaps up to a billion people affected ... coastal flooding ..."

Seager made the interesting argument that 2 degrees of warming might actually have some early benefits for people in Europe and North America, e.g. greater crop yields, or reduced heating costs.

> Seager: "[T]he 2 degrees bandwagon ... really reflects a confidence that climate change is mostly going to happen to *them* — at least it's going to happen to *them* first ... it sets a tolerance level for human-caused death ... we're going to be ok except for those 40 million people over there who aren't ok ... that is stunningly disconnected from things environmental ... throwing overboard the

tropical forests, the corals … this is not a target that's framed with anything like an environmental mindset."

"[I]f you look at the models … about 2 degrees is when *them* becomes *us*" [author's emphasis].

She also pointed out the error in scientific thinking that any such goal, 2 degrees or otherwise, reveals:

Seager: "To say 2 degrees kind of gives this impression of precision … this impression that it's drawn from science and science models … it reveals this extraordinary hubris … it frames the Earth as an oven … as a system that we can master …

"The Earth is not like an oven that you can turn on to 350 degrees and then turn it off (laughter from audience)."

In fall 2018, the UN Intergovernmental Panel on Climate Change released a grim study of global conditions and the head of the World Meterological Society, Petteri Taalas, supported Seager's point: "What is the difference between 1.5 degree and 2 degree? And one of the major issues is that there would be **420 million people less suffering because of climate change**, if we would be able to limit the warming to 1.5 degree …" [author's emphasis].

## *Celebrating Rachel Carson*

This observation on scientific hubris is informed by Seager's close reading of and commentary on Rachel Carson's *Silent Spring*, a book which burst onto the popular science scene in 1962 and gave birth to the U.S. environmental movement as we know it. In 2014 Bloomsbury published Seager's *Carson's Silent Spring: A Reader's Guide*. Seager characterized Carson's approach to her study of the world:

> "... as a scientist, [Carson] argued the necessity of incorporating humility and a sense of wonder into modern science. Readers and reviewers may have mistaken Carson's lyrical and gentle approach to her subject as a lesser science, but to the contrary, for her, this was the only scientifically responsible approach to apprehending a delicately balanced web of life shaped by forces too large to comprehend with mere scientific instruments ..."

Carson's approach to science embraced humility, a sense of wonder, and a certainty that "man" could not and should not control nature.

Over 50 years after this breakthrough text appeared, Seager's *Guide* is the first book to analyze *Silent Spring*'s lasting influence on the environmental movement, and to contextualize it for a new audience. This is the kind of reinforcement that male scientists and authors often receive, but which is rare for women intellectuals.

## *Critiquing the "Mother Earth" Metaphor*

Ecofeminism in Seager's view dictates understanding nature, not imposing one's will on it, or indulging in sentimentality. She is critical of the metaphor of "Mother Earth" and especially the wish fulfillment expressed as in "Mother Nature will save us," as explained in her 1994 book *Earth Follies: Coming to Feminist Terms with the Global Environmental Crisis*.

In 2001, in *Putting Women In Place: Feminist Geographers Make Sense of the World*, Seager and co-author Mona Domosh reference the "'Mom will pick up after us' school of environmental philosophy" and its implications for pollution as described by Linda Weitner in a 1989 piece in the *Boston Globe*:

> "Men are the ones who imagine that clean laundry gets into their drawers as if by magic, that muddy footprints evaporate into thin air ... It's these over-indulged and over-aged boys who operate on the assumption that disorder — spilled oil, radioactive wastes, plastic debris — is someone else's worry ..."

The contemporary environmental justice movement rejects hierarchies, and opposes the racist policies and practices that privilege the people who live in what Seager described as "our kind of latitude" over people who live nearer the equator, or white people who live in gated communities far from pollution sources over people of color who live in subsidized public housing.

## The United Nations and Gender Issues

UNESCO and the United Nations Environmental Programme (UNEP) have long engaged Seager's skills and knowledge as a consultant to integrate gender issues into UN environmental analyses and disaster relief projects.

Seager served, with other, mostly women experts, as Lead Writer for the 2016 Global Gender and Environment Outlook (GGEO) which is "the world's first comprehensive, integrated and global assessment about gender and the environment." This detailed report responded to the demands of an international group of women ministers of the environment, as well as decades-long, women-centric environmental campaigns, such as the Chipko movement to protect forests in India, and the Kenyan Green Belt movement led by Nobel Laureate Wangari Maathai. The press release for the GGEO stated, "It will provide governments and other stakeholders with the evidence-based global and regional information, data, and tools they need for transformational, gender-responsive environmental policy-making – *if they're willing to do so*" (authors' emphasis). Its chapters analyze the issues of water collection, food security or the lack of it, forests, oceans, sanitation and more, as they impact, in different ways, women and men, boys and girls. Flashes of Seager's characteristic wit come through the massive text, as in "the need to lift the roof off the household" to determine changes in who's doing which chores [such as collecting water and firewood] in developing countries.

The list of her presentations to United Nations' conferences is long: "Water governance, gender and development: conceptual challenges & data collection" for UNESCO in Italy in 2014; the UNEP's UN Second Environment Assembly (Nairobi) Network of Women Ministers in 2016; and the UN's African Women & Energy Entrepreneurship Network in 2017, to name only three. COP22 (the U.N.'s International Climate Change Meetings) in Morocco in 2016 saw her join many women activists and leaders in an unprecedented focus "on gendered effects of climate change, its mitigation and adaptation."

A key issue in Seager's work is the need for separating out information on how men and women are impacted by natural disasters, genocides, and wars. Without sex-disaggregated data (data collected and stored separately on males and females), the different consequences faced by women and girls disappear into generalizations that prevent governments and NGOs from applying resources where they are most needed.

## "The Connections Between and Among Women"

Seager's activism started when she was working as a young feminist in the bookstore New Words: A Women's Bookstore in Somerville, Massachusetts. Her scholarship has long centered the conditions of women, grounded in the place- and space-based discipline of geography. Her body of work is formidable: author or co-author of 9 books; editor of *A Companion to Feminist Geography*; and author of hundreds of articles, including numerous pieces for the general public in the now-defunct *Village Voice*.

At a tribute at MIT to the late poet Adrienne Rich in 2012, Mistress of Ceremony Seager quoted Rich's observation that "the connections between and among women are the most feared, the most problematic, and the most potentially transforming force on the planet."

Added Seager: "It's a mantra for our times."

## Analysis

Despite having written and spoken about environmental issues for decades, Professor Seager's expertise is not featured on either alternative news programs such as *Democracy Now!*, or mainstream TV shows such as Anderson Cooper's *360 Degrees* on CNN. Part of Seager's relative public obscurity, notwithstanding her professional success as an academic, author and consultant, can also be traced to the anti- or non-intellectual tendencies in North American media and society. With the exceptions of (male) scientists with TV shows, such as Carl Sagan, Bill Nye, and Neil Degrasse Tyson, the public rarely gets to know the personalities and work of scientists of any field. Scientists as a group are satirized — and trivialized — in films such as the popular *Back to the Future* movies and TV shows such as *The Big Bang Theory*.

Ask a college-educated adult to name a geographer, and she or he will most likely name Amerigo Vespucci. It helps to have your (slightly altered) first name given to two continents! Or the image, if not the name, that comes to mind might well be that of "The Geographer" painted by Dutch artist Johannes Vermeer.

Maybe geography is a field that most people don't see as important. How about public health and the viability of a municipal water supply? Ongoing lead poisoning in babies and children? Maybe those are areas where a woman's outstanding work is more likely to be recognized.

# CHAPTER EIGHT

# Corrosion of Trust: MONA HANNA-ATTISHA (b.1976)

*"We fought back with science."*

It was 2017, and the so-called Muslim ban on immigration to the U.S. was on. In "Corroding the American Dream," a researcher and pediatrician born in England whose parents emigrated from Iraq penned an op-ed for *The New York Times*:

> "… everyone in this country, except for Native Americans, came from somewhere else. Many of us were fleeing something, or were brought here by force in America's original sin. As an immigrant who holds a medical degree, I'm in good company. The organization that accredits graduate medical training programs says that there are more than 10,000 licensed physicians in the United States who graduated from medical

school in the seven countries the president listed in his travel ban …

"There are little girls who look just like I did at that age, who see their place in the American dream fading away, which makes me wonder what we all stand to lose."

Thus wrote Dr. Mona Hanna-Attisha of Flint, Michigan.

Ever heard of her?

## *Easy Research, Troubling Findings*

Ironically, Dr. Mona (as she's generally called) is not Muslim. Her Arabic name aside, she's the daughter of dissident scientists who fled the torture regime of Saddam Hussein. After a brief stay in England, the Hannas settled in Michigan, where they raised their daughter in their Chaldean Christian faith. They sent her to public schools, including the University of Michigan, where she earned a degree in environmental health, and Michigan State University College of Human Medicine. She is now an associate professor of pediatrics. When she married Dr. Elliott Attisha, another pediatrician, she hyphenated her name and that of their two daughters. Would she be allowed to immigrate to the U.S. today?

Dr. Mona's major accomplishment is rooted in a tragedy still unfolding today: lead poisoning caused by pollution of the public water supply in Flint, Michigan. She began studying lead levels in children after Elin Warn Betanzo, a former EPA employee who was a friend from high school, mentioned over dinner that Professor Marc Edwards at Virginia Tech had found high levels of lead in homes in Flint. Dr. Mona used hospital records for her research after the State of Michigan refused to respond to her requests for data. The poisoning had begun in 2014 when Darnell Earley, an unelected emergency manager appointed by Governor Rick Snyder, tried to save money by sourcing the public water supply from the polluted, corrosive Flint River — a truth the city, county and state found very inconvenient.

Calling her study "the easiest research project I have ever done" Dr. Mona explained why in an interview on TV show *Democracy Now!*:

> "We routinely screen children for lead at the ages of one and at ages of two. Medicaid children, who are on public insurance, are recommended to get lead screenings. So we had the data ...
>
> "So all we did was go back and look at our data. And we compared the percentage of children with elevated lead levels before the water switch, which was 2013, to 2015, and that water switch happened in 2014."

At a press conference on September 24, 2015, Dr. Mona announced her team's research findings before they were peer reviewed. The study results she shared revealed that Flint children's blood lead levels had doubled or even tripled after April 2014. She later explained her decision:

> "We shared these results at a press conference, and you don't usually share research at press conferences. It's supposed to be shared in published medical journals, which now it is.
>
> "But we had an ethical, moral, professional responsibility to alert our community about this crisis, this emergency."

As journalists recorded, she urged the people of Flint —
particularly families with children — to stop drinking the
water, and especially stop using it to make infant formula,
a practice she had formerly okayed and now felt terribly
guilty about. The very next day the city of Flint issued a
health advisory warning, and at the state capital in Lansing
demonstrators began clamoring for Governor Snyder's
resignation over the scandal.

But, state health officials initially belittled Dr. Mona's
research, and she went to bed the night of the press conference
feeling like throwing up.

> Hanna-Attisha: "I was called an 'unfortunate
> researcher,' that I was causing near hysteria, that
> I was splicing and dicing numbers, and that the
> state data was not consistent with my data. And
> as a scientist, as a researcher, as a professional,
> you double-check and you triple-check, and the
> numbers didn't lie. And we knew that. But when
> the state, with a team of like 50 epidemiologists,
> tells you you're wrong, you second-guess
> yourself. But that lasted just a short period, and
> we regrouped and told them why, 'No, you were
> wrong.'
>
> "And after about a week and a half or two weeks,
> after some good conversations, they relooked
> at their numbers and finally said that the state's
> findings were consistent with my findings."

### *Setting the Record Straight*

A subsequent press conference in January, 2016 convened
by federal Environmental Protection Agency (EPA) officials
to "rebuild trust" shows Dr. Mona looking skeptical as an

acting administrator, hastily appointed to replace a regional administrator who resigned, speaks.

Governor Rick Snyder appointed Dr. Mona to three public health commissions formed after she uncovered the Flint water crisis. *Democracy Now!*'s Amy Goodman commented about watching a viral clip from that press conference, one where Dr. Mona joined Snyder and state health officials at the podium, but "you were shaking your head 'no,' right there in the frame, standing behind the government health officials. You were supposed to be standing with them, and you were shaking your head 'no.'"

Dr. Mona explained:

> "Yes. So, I am willing to work with anybody for the benefit of children, and I was at that press conference with the governor and with state health officials, who we are working with now.
>
> "However, they said that only 43 people since October had elevated lead levels! And it really minimizes this population-wide exposure. This is an entire population who was exposed to this neurotoxin. So when you say these small numbers, it just — once again, the population loses trust in government and in their ability to protect people."

Dr. Mona's 2018 book about the crisis, *What The Eyes Don't See: A Story of Crisis, Resistance, and Hope in an American City,* brought her widespread publicity with appearances on mainstream media including the *PBS News Hour* and *Time Magazine. Eyes* was one of the top picks for summer on Oprah. com where it was described as "revealing, with the gripping intrigue of a Grisham thriller." It had already been optioned by a Hollywood production company by the time it was released in June 2018.

Her 2017 TEDMED talk has been viewed on YouTube by thousands of people, and she has competed for a children's charity on the game show "Who Wants To Be A Millionaire?" in addition to receiving many awards.

## *Rallying Support*

When not on the celebrity author circuit, Dr. Mona serves as the director of Hurley Hospital's Pediatric Residency program and of the Pediatric Public Health Initiative, a partnership between Hurley Medical Center and Michigan State University aimed at improving wellness for people in Flint who were exposed to lead in high concentrations. She also is a founding donor of the Flint Child and Health Development Fund, established to address the health impacts that will unfold over the next several decades for those exposed to lead in early childhood.

Dr. Mona cites a host of collaborators and a long list of mentors to explain how she was able to take on the State of Michigan and win. She is quick to give credit to the water engineers, researchers, hospital administrators, elected officials, software wizards, and publicity experts who teamed up to prove the harmful effects of sending lead-polluted water into the homes of the children of Flint. They were careful to protect their data and identities while they raced to solve the puzzle; the doctor with the *nom de guerre* "Fire Ant" wrote in *Eyes*, "I was just the last piece." As an individual, she cites a family history of left activism and pro-democracy organizing, even whistleblowing, that stretches back several generations, a legacy that is actively passed down to the children.

Giving credit to the American Dream her immigrant parents were chasing, Dr. Mona acknowledges the excellent public school and university education she received, and the strong influence of her high school environmental action peers and mentors. She also cites many activists from the past who inspired her: health reformer Alice Hamilton and labor leader Genora Johnson Dollinger among them. When she re-tells the family story to her daughters of how her grandfather had his broken leg mended in Iraq, "I always say she's a lady doctor."

The last chapter in *Eyes* is a satisfyingly long list of the public health officials who either resigned or were removed; some of them even faced criminal charges, including manslaughter and felonies related to the cover-up. The EPA administrator for Region 5 resigned, the mayor lost his re-election bid, and the governor — eventually offering what Dr. Mona considered a sincere apology — did not make an expected run for the White House. This is fitting for a book whose theme is the failure of democracy under unelected emergency managers of Flint appointed by the governor but not accountable to the people. Protesters crop up often in *Eyes*, and more than once Dr. Mona wishes she was outside with them instead of inside with the suits.

Census figures show 40% percent of Flint residents have incomes below the federal poverty line, and 54% are black. Dr. Mona noted in her book that the American Dream has been denied to many of her patients and their families, and argued,

> "there really are two Americas, aren't there? The one I was lucky enough to grow up in, and the other America — the one I see in my clinic every day ... Too many kids are growing up in a nation that does not value their future, or even try to offer them one."

She considers the report eventually published by a blue-ribbon task force appointed by the governor "historic -- never had a government report explicitly stated the role of race in an environmental crisis." According to Dr. Mona, "A person living in Flint right now has a 15-year less life expectancy than a person in a neighboring zip code. We all know that this would not have happened in a richer city. It would not have happened in a whiter city."

## *Analysis*

Will her momentary fame endure, or will it evaporate like that of so many accomplished women of the past? Will another health crusader's book someday be described as having the gripping intrigue of a Dr. Mona thriller? She noted with delight that media reports on the Flint crisis started out describing her as a "local pediatrician" before transitioning to "hospital researcher." In the face of pseudo-science from public health officials who continued to claim the water was safe long after she had proved it wasn't, she was gratified to confront the public relations man from the governor's office who had called her study "unfortunate" and the classic sexist taunt, "hysterical." Turns out, it was unfortunate indeed — for him, because he lost his job.

Dr. Mona is the woman most likely to succeed in being too famous for this book. But despite her many appearances in television news and commentary and her op-eds in mainstream publications, we're guessing you still didn't know her name. "Oh, yes, that doctor in Flint," is the most common response you might hear. Being a woman of color is already a major step to being invisible in the mainstream. Having an Arabic name may contribute to memory problems in a culture where many insist that everyone "should speak American." Or maybe it's mostly that she's still quite young. We're guessing she'll continue pushing vigorously at the barriers that prevent her young patients from enjoying good health and normal developmental milestones, and maybe someday most people in the U.S. will be able to say they have heard of her.

What about women working to advocate for a quarter of a million women who were kept as sex slaves by an invading army? The United Nations recognizes sexual enslavement is a war crime, and a sex slave who escaped and now advocates for other women and girls, Nadia Murad, was recently awarded the Nobel Peace Prize. Would a woman whose life work is struggling against those who would silence such women and deny their suffering be well-known today?

# CHAPTER NINE

# For the Grandmothers:
# PHYLLIS KIM (b.1969)

*"To prevent the same atrocity from repeating."*

Phyllis Kim didn't set out to cause a rift between major cities on the Pacific Rim, but in part because of her efforts, San Francisco and Osaka are no longer sister cities. In 2017 San Francisco installed a monument to remember the "comfort women," approximately 200,000 young women, primarily from Korea, China, and the Philippines, who were enslaved to provide sex for Japanese troops before and during WWII. The mayor of Osaka threatened San Francisco with severance of their relationship if the memorial was accepted, and a struggle ensued. As executive director of the Korean American Forum of California (KAFC), Kim had already collaborated in the successful effort to install a similar monument — also vehemently opposed by the Japanese government — in the

Los Angeles suburb of Glendale. A busy court interpreter, Kim nevertheless found time to travel north to San Francisco every month to help human trafficking survivors who she believes deserve to be remembered.

Ever heard of her?

## *The Courage To Speak*

The survivors' stories of atrocity were whispered in the night to a mother or a sister, revisited in nightmares, and locked in the heart for decades. It seemed their lives would end without justice or healing, and this vast crime, spanning 23 countries in East Asia, would go unrecorded in official histories. And yet ... at first Korean survivor Kim Hak-sun, then others, found the courage to speak in public about their enslavement and rape, and demand a formal apology from the Japanese government.

These elderly women are tenderly and respectfully called "Grandma" by their supporters, although most were too damaged to marry and have children. Their testimonies have now been recorded on video, in scholarly articles and books, and represented in artwork. Much of this desire for justice came in the context of he 1980s-1990s pro-democracy movement in South Korean society, which included feminism.

The ongoing, international movement for justice for military sex slaves and an honest record of this bitter history is led mostly by women. They support the few remaining "Grandmas," organize memorials, continue research, and do media outreach and public education work.

Installing memorial statuary is just one piece of the remembering work that Kim and the KAFC have pursued. But, it may be the most important. She explained:

"A memorial in a public place is easily used for public education. It represents public opinion within a city, and the approval of the city government. It can reach an indefinite number of people over time.

"I think it's the power of the memorials that the Japanese government is the most afraid of. I think the memorials are effective. The art says a thousand words."

## *"Comfort Women"*

Born in Seoul, South Korea, Kim immigrated, with her family, to California in 1990, attending community college and then UCLA. Growing up in South Korea, Kim had always known about the issue but had not been involved previously. Her maternal grandmother had been "married off early to avoid conscription" by the occupying Japanese Army. "Everyone knows," said Kim, "because of their knowledge of the Japanese occupation [of Korea]. In the late '80s, there was a TV soap opera about the so-called 'comfort women.' It was a great hit."

She became motivated to remember the history of wartime sex crimes when she learned of Japanese-American Congressman Michael Honda's bill, House Resolution 121, to recognize the "comfort women." H.Res. 121 reads: "A resolution expressing the sense of the House of Representatives that the Government of Japan should formally acknowledge, apologize, and accept historical responsibility in a clear and unequivocal manner for its Imperial Armed Forces' coercion of young women into sexual slavery, known to the world as 'comfort women,' during its colonial and wartime occupation of Asia and the Pacific Islands from the 1930s through the duration of World War II" and it passed in 2007. It calls on Japan to ...

> "(1) formally acknowledge, apologize, and accept historical responsibility for its Imperial Armed Force's coercion of young women into sexual slavery (comfort women) during its colonial and wartime occupation of Asia and the Pacific Islands from the 1930s through the duration of World War II; (2) have this official and public apology presented by the Prime Minister of Japan; (3) refute any claims that the sexual enslavement and trafficking of the comfort women never occurred; and (4) educate current and future generations about this crime while following the international community's recommendations with respect to the comfort women."

The government of Japan has thus far done none of these things.

Kim noted of Honda's effort, "He said that he was doing this for Japan, so that Japan wouldn't repeat the same mistakes. That was really striking to me." (*Note: Rep. Michael Honda of California was interned as an infant by the U.S. in camps set up to detain Japanese and Japanese-Americans during the war.*)

## *Breaking the Silence*

As part of the campaign to create a memorial in San Francisco, Kim met one of the few remaining South Korean survivors. Breaking the silence around victimization that brought shame in addition to intense suffering, survivor Lee Yong-soo spent a month in California in 2007. In an interview, Kim spoke of "Grandma" Lee:

> "I was her scheduler and interpreter and driver, spending all day with her ...

"What struck me was that she's been on this speaking tour in several countries, but the pain she goes through every time she recounts what happened ... If I were in her shoes, would I have that strength to do that — not once, but twice, 10 times, 20 times? It was amazing."

The testimonies are indeed grim. Breaking their silence in old age, survivors have come forward to recount what happened to them. For most, they were in their early teens when a false promise of work lured them to "factories" that turned out to be forced sex camps. There they were kept under armed guard, raped up to 50 times a day by Japanese soldiers, beaten, and threatened with death. They were forced to have abortions and endured ghastly treatments for sexually transmitted diseases. Many attempted or committed suicide, and some were executed as a way of hiding the crimes committed against them.

The denial of their experiences has prolonged their suffering. During a meeting of the San Francisco board of supervisors, following Lee Yong-soo's testimony a Japanese-American man called her a "liar" and a "prostitute." The Japanese government has yet to take official responsibility or make a governmental apology, as opposed to a personal apology, which the survivors condemn as utterly inadequate and missing the point of their struggle. Spokespeople for the Japan government have at times denied the existence of "comfort women" or, more often, claimed that they were prostitutes who were well-compensated. A private donor in Japan offered compensatory payments to survivors, but many of them refused the money. "It is impossible to compensate me. All I want is an apology," said survivor Lei Gui-Ying.

Japanese media is full of false reports that the South Korean government agreed to remove a highly controversial memorial in front of Japan's consulate in Seoul, and this has confused many in Japan who were not even alive during WWII. The control of information, at least in Japan, appears to have been successful; many Japanese young people interviewed knew little about the "comfort women" but did believe that the South Korean government had backed down from its promise. The Japanese government reportedly has a budget of $500 million annually to fight "comfort women" memorials around the world.

### *Who Writes the History?*

Not surprisingly, Kim has gotten involved in so-called "History Wars" around what will be taught in California public schools about the realities of WWII. Her organization was successful in advocating for the inclusion of "comfort women" in guidelines adopted in 2016, intended for use by textbook publishers. According to a report in the *Los Angeles Times*:

> "Bill Honig, co-chair of the History-Social Science subject matter committee, said they consulted the latest historical research and survivors' testimony and concluded there was enough evidence for it to be taught in schools.
>
> "Honig said he believed the issue would be a valuable starting point for students to research and discuss the present-day problem of human trafficking."

Connecting history to current issues is a best practice in social studies education, especially for adolescents, many of whom can relate to being the same age as the conscripted "comfort women." And because California schools are such a large market for textbooks, their content influences the content of textbooks in other states.

"Remembering and honoring the Grandmas is a way to empower the victims of sexual violence then and in the present time," wrote Phyllis Kim in a Comfort Women Justice campaign email. Her work is reminiscent of the #MeToo movement, which has seen many survivors of sexual violence come forward with their stories. But Kim thinks there is a crucial element missing: "#MeToo doesn't show the context ... the focus is on celebrities, and everyday sexual violence against women is not being addressed." With women and girls continuing to be sexually assaulted as a consequence and even a tactic in wars raging around the globe today, Kim's work to support survivors and their stories is crucial. "Many younger women identify the issue as their own," she told us. "They are most touched by the courage of the Grandmas to speak out."

The yearly commemoration in Glendale is an exemplary instance of "memory work." The city government officials involved in approving the memorial were honored and invited to talk about their motivations, which included the empathy of the then-mayor, an Armenian-American. Faith leaders, members of the large local Korean-American community, reporters and photographers, and the general public were welcomed. In the adjacent city library, a two-part exhibit displayed videos of the survivors giving testimony and large photos of current activism in South Korea. This event interwove solemn with less formal elements: a communal meal; singing by a Korean choral group; a poster contest involving youth from middle and high schools in the area; speeches; and Kim's announcement of a new public education campaign.

# *Analysis*

The Comfort Women Justice Movement is different from the other stories in *Ever Heard of Her?* This movement confronts the determined attempt by members of a hostile government and right-wing organizations to censor — indeed, to literally remove — memorials to a history of war crimes against women, not only in their own country, but in other countries as well. We selected Phyllis Kim as one of a number of women leaders in this international movement. (We might have selected scholar Miho Lee Kim, an ethnic Korean raised as a non-citizen in Japan, or retired Judge Julie Tang, a Chinese-American, or white American attorney Judith Mirkinson, president of the San Francisco-based Comfort Women Justice Coalition, or many others.) It is not surprising that a lead organizer of a justice movement is not well-known outside of activist networks, but it is striking that the movement itself is not better known to the general American public.

One part of the relative obscurity of this movement may be that it centers the history of East Asian women. Retired Judge Lillian Sing told *The New Yorker* that "she felt that racism in the United States had played a silencing role when it comes to recognizing what happened to the comfort women. 'Why did this take so long?' she said."

Another factor may be that the women being remembered were victims of **sex** crimes, a topic for pornography and prurient titillation in popular culture, not for legal redress and serious scholarship and commemoration — until recently.

However, the indirect influence of the "Grandmas" who began speaking up a generation ago, in the face of intense cultural taboos and their own shame, is shown in recent events. A survivor of the same war crimes — abduction and sexual slavery by enemies of her people — Nadia Murad, a Yazidi Iraqi-Kurdish young woman, was awarded the 2018 Nobel Peace Prize. Along with her co-laureate, physician Denis Mukwege, who helps the victims of sexual violence in the Democratic Republic of Congo, Murad testifies publicly to the profound injustice of these crimes. Murad and Mukwege were given this highest peace award a decade after the United Nations recognized "the use of sexual violence as a weapon of war."

The "Grandmas" have frequently said that they do this work of remembering so that no one will suffer as they did. Sadly, the crimes of sexual slavery as a war tactic continue — but the survivors are often able to speak out far sooner, and receive support more quickly, than did the women of East Asia raped by the Japanese military. Shame is replaced by the demand for justice.

In statues, high school textbooks, video testimonies, magazine articles and other media, the unspeakable has become the spoken. The violent acts against women's bodies which perpetrators wish to commit and then forget, evading all consequences, have entered international law and the historical record.

Phyllis Kim translated the softly spoken words of survivors — and the world has heard, and will not forget.

# Conclusion

## "We've Heard of Her!" Making Recognition Happen

*"When the whole world is silent, even one voice becomes powerful." - Malala Yousafzi*

Now that you've heard of our nine women of achievement, you're probably thinking: What about _____ ? Why wasn't she included?

This is a good thing!

Imagine how difficult it was to select just nine women to feature. Even limiting the field to women who achieved in the U.S. there were dozens of women who could have been included.

For example:

The Black Lives Matter movement opposing police brutality was founded in 2013 by Alicia Garza, Patrisse Khan-Cullors, and Opal Tometi. The high rate of police killings of unarmed BIPOC Americans continues to make this one of the most urgent social change projects of the century. The focus on often-overlooked women, including transwomen, who are victims of police violence, is expressed poignantly in the enduring hashtag #SayHerName.

Indigenous women lead environmental and climate justice campaigns. Tara Houska, Winona LaDuke, and Cheri Honkala are a few names among many who bring forward the wisdom of Native culture about how to live sustainably on what is now called the United States. Their wisdom, courage, and long-standing dedication to their lands and peoples are models for non-indigenous eco-activists.

The MeToo movement calling out sexual harassment and assault by powerful men was initiated in 2006 by community organizer Tarana Burke, who works with rape victims. Powerful men have been outed, fired, and (in too few cases) charged with crimes. Celebrity women who came late to the movement got more attention than Burke, a Black woman, but if this were a longer book she is the one who most deserves to be included.

Grief-stricken, fired-up mothers by the thousands have joined Moms Demand Action nationwide since 2012. The Moms demand common sense gun control and an end to the horror of massacres in public schools. After the slaughter of 14 students and 3 teachers at Margery Stoneman Douglas High School in Florida, the inspired activism of surviving students like passionately articulate teen Emma Gonzalez carried forward the movement to end mass killings by gun lobby-enabled extremists.

The list of women who could have been included is a long one. And, the project of finding and celebrating their achievements goes on!

We invite you to help us center marginalized voices at our website, EverHeardOfHer.com. Transwomen and underage women are welcome. Nominate your friend, your teacher, your faith leader, or your coach. Help us write the sequel so that more and more people can read it and say: "We've heard of her!"

# Acknowledgements

Many thanks to the living women of achievement who are included in this book. To Simone Browne, Phyllis Kim, Dr. Mona Hana-Attisha, Joni Seager, and Ann Wright: your achievements and hard work continue to astonish and inspire me.

I owe a great debt to two partners in this book project: Pat Taub, who had the original idea and got us started, and Janet Weil, who believed in the idea and did the lioness' share of the research. Janet also read my drafts, argued our thesis, and generally kept me going through the process of turning an idea into a book.

I am grateful to the many family members who encouraged and supported the book project. They reviewed and shared iterations of the "ever heard of her?" lists of names, made suggestions of overlooked women of achievement, and cheered me on.

Librarians too numerous to mention helped as well. The Portland (OR) State University library, Colby College art library, and several public libraries helped cast the net wide for women of accomplishment and drill down to find their own words to include in this book.

To the Pfeifle family: Sam, who carried the project over the production finish line; Hannah, who helped him; and Ruby, who created excellent illustrations of the women.

To the many, many people who perused lists of possible women to include and returned them with some version of, "I am embarrassed to say I have never heard of any of these women" — thank you! You were instrumental in helping identify women who were not well-known but certainly deserve to be.

Special researcher thanks to Robert Weil and John Weil for general cheerleading; Debbie O'Flynn and Jeffrey O'Flynn (source material for Florence Price); Sue Anderson of the Osher Lifelong Learning Institute at California State University, Palm Desert ("beta-testing" of the concept and some material for a summer 2018 adult ed class Janet taught); and Miho Kim Lee (Comfort Women Justice movement, Koreans in Japan, and Phyllis Kim — tremendously helpful!).

And finally, to the younger generations: May you be able to name, not only the first Black woman to win an Olympic gold medal for the United States, but the names of many other women whose accomplishments are deserving of our attention. I wrote this book for you.